Spiritual Warfare

for the

Not So Swift

Advantage
INSPIRATIONAL

D. M. Carthern

First Printing: January 2007
07 08 09 10 11 12 13   9 8 7 6 5 4 3 2 1
Printed in the United States of America

Introduction

I was minding my own business one day, when I accidentally bumped into a hornet's nest (*in the spiritual sense*) and 14 months later ended the most intense trial that I had ever been through. All I did was give a C.S. Lewis book (*Mere Christianity*) to a manager at work who said that she was studying the great religions of the world. That was the equivalent of giving a Bible commentary to one of Satan's top generals, only I did not know that at the time. I was just trying to help. By the time that trial was finished, I finally knew what that scripture 'being crucified with Christ' was all about.

For most of my walk, I had carefully sidestepped that part about picking up my cross and dying to myself. I don't know why I thought that I could outsmart God, but I did often wonder how He was going to complete His work with me. Of course, that was His problem, not mine. As I found out, He never did consider that a problem.

I am sure, or I certainly hope, He completed the bulk of His work with me in that trial. He went into areas that I had closed off since childhood. It seemed that there was no corner that He was not going to touch with that trial. I have never had such agonizing pain in my life. When the trial was over, I clearly knew the spiritual benefits that I had reaped from it, but oh my! I would never choose to go through that trial again but, even *I* have to admit the Lord accomplished years of work in a short amount of

time. Afterwards, I started thinking that if people knew a few basics of spiritual warfare, maybe they could avoid some of the snares that I stepped into.

Actually, the truth is that I got so mad at myself for being so obtuse and the enemy for being so cruel that I thought I would enlighten my fellow brothers and sisters to his ugly schemes.

I say this book is for the not so swift because this is a book for Christians that just don't get it unless it is right in front of them. Most of these spiritual truths and principles I just didn't get until I was hit over the head with them for years and then it would suddenly dawn on me. I just assumed that I was not the only Christian like that. Right?

If you are like most Christians, myself included, spiritual warfare is a subject that is read about in books. Sometimes you occasionally hear teachings about it. For the more serious Christian you even go to conferences and buy books on the subject. It usually lingers in the mind as something to be on guard about and it has something to do with demons. Usually, those "deeper" saints talk about it a lot. For the most part the general Christian populace does not have a clue about spiritual warfare. This book is an effort to spell out the basics for any and all Christians. Whether we know it or not, whether we acknowledge it or not, whether we believe it or not, we are deeply involved in spiritual warfare. We are in the war every minute of every day. Most of us are walking casualties.

We have been casualties for so long that we think we are living the normal Christian life. If you think that you have heard it all before and it has not driven you into a deeper walk with the Captain, you are a casualty on the sidelines. I used to think that being on the sidelines was okay and I would just bide my time until the Lord came. Fortunately for myself and other saints, the Lord will not tolerate slackers. His kingdom suffers violence for only a season.

This is not a book of condemnation. This is a book of wisdom for those who have ears to hear. I will not bog you down with a bunch of nebulous theories or scare tactics. I do not believe that there is a demon or a demon strategy behind everything that goes wrong in our lives. Often, we lay out our own snares and without any help from anyone, we step into them. Often, we are the casualties of demon strategies. It takes a relationship with the Captain to know which is which and what our next move needs to be. The Lord was absolutely serious when He said that we are "more than conquerors." We are not to be the walking wounded or the cowering cowards. If we are to be obedient saints, the Lord says quite forcefully, "Stop regarding man, whose breath of life is in his nostrils; for why should he be esteemed?" Is.2: 22

Fear not, this is not a book to kick the saints, quite the opposite. It is a book to remind you or inform you of who you are *if you have been born again.* You are the son or the daughter of the Lord of Hosts, the Almighty, and the One True Living God. **The demons should tremble.** Living in us is the Maker of all things, why do we fear? We fear because we know zip about spiritual warfare and how unrelenting our enemy is. We fear because we have not comprehended Who it is that we have a relationship with. When we *really* understand that "greater is He that is in us than he that is in the world," **the demons will tremble.** We can continue getting beat up or we can finally stand up, take our shield and sword and start to do some serious offensive battle. We were called to be saints; all of the great saints had to learn to battle skillfully. And you will, too.

D.M. Carthern

Table of Contents

Chapter One

The Lay of the Land

Therefore, prepare your minds for action, keep sober in spirit, fix your hope completely on the grace to be brought to you at the revelation of Jesus Christ.1 Pet. 1:13

We read, we pray, we tithe, and we get attacked. When we can get our senses to work again, we realize that we are in for a bad day. Maybe you are the optimistic sort, "Well, praise God." Neither view is correct. Picture a soldier in a war and he has guard duty for the unit. Would we think it normal for a soldier to *not* react to a bullet whizzing by his head? Would we think it normal for the soldier to say a cheerful 'oh well, praise God,' when the bullet had lodged in the doorpost next to him instead of his head? Wouldn't we think it was more appropriate for him to dive to the ground and seek cover? He would then begin looking to see where the attack came from and also to warn his unit that they, *not just him*, are under attack. Beloved, we need to be soldiers. We are really in a war. The enemy really is trying to kill us.

As much as we desire to just go about our business, the fact is that we cannot; we are not civilians. Most soldiers do not desire for a war to happen. They prepare for the war but they do not desire war. We need to prepare and prepare in such a way that when the attack happens our constant drilling just takes over.

Our mind must be in the alert mode, we must never forget that we are in hostile territory. Our enemy will attack day or night, or day <u>and</u> night. For those of us thinking that our walk does not warrant this kind of attention, *that* thinking alone shows that you have already been hit. If you tithe, go to church faithfully, you might even be a deacon, your kids and spouse love you, if you are not conscious of the warfare going on in your life, you have been hit. No one gets a free ride; no one gets to dodge the war. You are either in the heat of the battle or you are a casualty.

If we have not acknowledged that we are sinners, repented of our sins, accepted Jesus as our Savior, allowed Him to be the Lord of our lives, we are casualties. You may be a good person, you may read the Bible everyday, you may fill your life with all kinds of good deeds, but you are still a casualty. You are the person who has no concept that a war even exists or who the players are, you are a definite casualty. Sorry. For those of us who have acknowledged that Jesus is our Savior and we have allowed Him to lead our lives, we are the ones who have an opportunity to wage a good fight.

If we are not absorbing the Word, we will get hit. If we do not pray without ceasing, we will get hit. If we do not nurture our relationship with Jesus, we will get hit. If we do all these things, we will definitely get hit! This is the first concept we must understand - we will get hit. When we get hit, it is not the end of the world, we have not failed the King and we are not worthless scum. Jesus, the Captain, got hit. The key to winning the battle is having a relationship with the Captain.

If we are not receiving our orders from Him, we will misinterpret a victory for a loss, or a loss for a victory. I don't think anyone would argue with me that if you look at Jesus' life and judge it by the usual standards of success – He was not a success. Most churches would not have had Him as an elder or pastor.

We have the mind of Christ. What does that mean when we are talking about spiritual warfare? Well, we do know He never let His guard down whether He was around family, friends or His enemies. He knew the attack could come at any time from anyone. Either He was very paranoid or a serious soldier. Your mentality must be that you are a soldier behind enemy lines. Any other mindset that you entertain will leave you a casualty. The enemy can use every human outside of the Kingdom of God to attack you. That leaves a lot of humans and a lot of human institutions.

Let's say you work in a corporation and you are moving up quickly. Senior management sees you as the next star on the horizon. You feel great, God is blessing you, and you work diligently in dedication to Him. You are not amazed that you are doing well at work since you work *as unto the Lord*. You have managed to cultivate some relationships with the senior management and you are quite comfortable in their presence. You share your thoughts, hopes and dreams concerning your career with some of the management people. They share their thoughts, hopes and dreams with you. You are careful not to mention your true source of life because that is against the rules of the corporation. But like any true saint, if *they* open the door you will not hesitate to take advantage of the opportunity to share the Good News. As time passes, the door opens and you share a little bit about Jesus. You are careful to not share more than they can handle, but the Seed goes out.

Unknown to you at the time, all of Hell is now aware that you are one of those Christians that *will* share the Gospel. Your co-workers that are not in the Kingdom are just pawns in the game. They do not have a clue as to what is really going on. They will believe that suddenly they cannot trust you because you are a bad person. The rumors about you are suddenly easy to believe. Many of your co-workers just down right hate you for no reason at all, and it seems good to them! Management blatantly lies about you and to you. Your fast rising star is falling fast. If this scenario catches you unawares, you have been hit.

A professing Christian is a Christian that will, out of necessity, learn to battle skillfully. The only ones that may even be aware that you are in a battle are you and the Captain. Your friends in the Kingdom may or may not be allowed to share in your battle; it all depends on what Jesus allows. He may use this to increase your skill level, or draw you closer to Him; the only way to find out will be in your relationship with Him. If you are like most Christians, you will run to the Rock as a last resort. You will try to reason through the situation. You will try to seek counsel from everybody but the Captain. You will seek comfort from everybody but Him. You will live with this gaping wound as long as you can until, finally, you come to the Rock.

You are a housewife and a mother of four beautiful children. Your spouse became a Christian while dating you. You always felt that he could press in a little deeper. He really has no clue as to what walking with the Lord is all about, anyway. You keep these thoughts to yourself. You dutifully make the best of this marriage because divorce is not an option. It is not an intimate, fun marriage but, for the kids sake, you continue to go to church and read and pray. In the meantime, your spouse hasn't felt the love of Christ from you in years, but he was never very sensitive to the Spirit anyway. One day you are driving around town doing errands with the kids in the car and your oldest child, who is six, says to you, "why don't you just get another husband?" Out of the mouth of babes, you have definitely been hit.

This could be a snare that you laid out for yourself or it could be a hit from the enemy. The only way to know is through your relationship with the Captain. If it was a snare you can be sure the Lord will help you deal with the issues that caused the snare. If it was a hit, the Lord will tend to your wound and tell you what to do next. You don't want to go running out in the field shooting blindly at anything that moves even though your pain will blind you momentarily. Remember, you are a soldier in battle; you must keep your wits about you. We need to get the strategy for our counter move and since we can't see our enemy, we need the Captain. We go to the Lord and press in deeper.

<u>Weapons</u>

The main weapons of the enemy are Depression, Denial, Sin, Fear, Delay and Pride. Of course the absence of constant self-evaluation will cut down a lot of the snares that we step into. I understand that there are many more weapons that the enemy will use, but really, the book could only be so long!

Depression: This will usually come after a great spiritual victory of some sort. I usually call it the enemy's backlash. The enemy will not tolerate *any* joy in your life. The saints that have learned the secret of praise know that the last thing the enemy wants is for you to give praise to the Lord when your world is falling down around you.

The benefit of praise is that it will take our eyes off of our troubles and ourselves and force us to concentrate on the Lord. It forces us to concentrate on something bigger than our self and our troubles. The Truth is allowed to seep in to our soul and we realize that "everything is going according to plan." When we lose sight of that truth, we become overwhelmed at the hopelessness of it all. Indeed, without the Lord in our lives, it is a hopeless situation –

that is the truth! The more we look at ourselves the lower we sink into depression.

The world is constantly sending out the message to self-evaluate. How are we doing? How do we look? How much do we weigh? Are our muscles big enough? Are our abs 'ripped' enough? What are we thinking? Are we in style? Ahead of the style? Last year's style? What are we planning? Are we planning enough? What is our intent? Our focus is always on me, me and me.

If we throw a dinner party for our friends, we need and wait for feedback, even if we disguise it as a concern for their welfare. Are you comfortable? Do you like the food? Do you need anything else? If everyone is comfortable, well fed and they have enjoyed good conversation, we receive the glory and we are quite content with ourselves. If everyone is comfortable, well fed and they have enjoyed good conversation except for that one person, we cannot let that go. Indeed, it might even lead us to be offended by that person. Why? They did not give us what *we* needed.

Isn't the world funny? The very counsel that they give, if followed, would lead us into deeper depression. But fear not! They have medication for that also. For those of us saints that are on medication for depression, please, ***do not be condemned!!***

The enemy would like to take this concept and run with it but lets not give him the opportunity or the satisfaction. I would just ask that we consider this possibility; if we are constantly looking at ourselves, after awhile it becomes a habit. Many habits affect us physically and mentally. If we are constantly praising God (*looking at Him*), after awhile it becomes a habit. Many habits affect us physically and mentally.

Denial: This is a tough one because we often deny that we do this; it causes a catch-22 situation. I will try to take a different angle than anticipated.

If the enemy can:

➢ Keep us from fully believing that we are loved
   Or that
➢ We are special
   Or that
➢ We are unique
   Or that
➢ We are more than conquerors
   Or that
➢ Our life is hid in Christ
   Or that
➢ Our treasure is in heaven
   Or that
➢ We are passing through
   Or that
➢ We are made new
   Or that
➢ We will see His face
   Or that
➢ We are accepted into the Beloved
   Or that
➢ We are accepted by Him
   Or that
➢ We are treasured by Him
   Or that
➢ *His desire* is for us

<u>Then</u> the enemy will ensnare us every time.

We are sons and daughters of the Living God, paid for with <u>His Son's</u> blood. Even in our darkened minds we understand that was a high price to pay for anybody. Most saints can read this paragraph and agree with it, mentally.

The problem that most of us have is believing that it pertains to each one of us, individually. We are in denial, we do not walk in the truth; we walk in a lie. Indeed, most of our walk is spent on grasping the concept that God loves us and called each one of us one at a time.

God has never lied. God never will lie. God does not struggle with not telling a lie. God does not imply a lie. God can be trusted.

For most humans, when we see a rainbow it causes us to pause and wonder at the beauty of it. Most humans do not remember the purpose of the rainbow. God remembers:

God said, "This is the sign of the covenant which I am making between Me an you, and every living creature that is with you, for all successive generations; I set My bow in the cloud, and it shall be for a sign of a covenant between Me and the earth. It shall come about, when I bring a cloud over the earth, that the bow will be seen in the cloud, and I will remember My covenant, which is between Me and you and every living creature of all flesh; and never again shall the water become a flood to destroy all flesh. When the bow is in the cloud, then I will look upon it, to remember the everlasting covenant between God and every living creature of all flesh that is on the earth." And God said to Noah, "This is the sign of the covenant which I have established between Me and all flesh that is on the earth." Gen.9: 12-17

It really does not matter if we remember the promises, God will still be faithful to the promises. He promises that if we repent and give our lives to Him, He will make us new and we will live forever. Whether we believe it or not deep down in our spirit, He will be faithful in carrying out that promise.

I think one of His favorite words must be 'Behold.' He says, "Behold, I make all things new." Each one of us is unique to God; He made us uniquely; that is why we all have different fingerprints. We are one of a kind. No one will ever be like you or me ever again. No one has ever been like you or me before us. He treasures our unique perspective on things. He enjoys the way we process data in our minds on the planet.

He desires to hear our unique voice in prayer. He delights to hear our unique voice in song and praise. The gifts and talents He has given you are for you alone. They were not left over items that He had on His heavenly shelf. He does not do *thrift*. These gifts and talents are for your personality that He made.

He desires to embrace your unique expression of the love you have for Him. No one can love Him the way you do. No one can love you like He does. You absolutely take His breath away. He has given up a Kingdom for you; He has given up His life for you. That is the truth that is often denied.

Sin: Lets talk about sin and why the Lord hates it so. Sin affected Lucifer, Adam and Eve. Adam and Eve infected the rest of the human race with it. We all can see its effects. Deeper than the physical effects are the spiritual effects. Prior to the fall, we as a species trusted God. We believed God. We praised God. We had fun *with* God. Our fall was so far down that now we wonder *how* God could possibly love us. We question God constantly and even when He answers our questions, we do not believe the answers. We doubt the Truth. Can you understand why He hates sin? Sin has put a natural distrust between Him and us.

Talking to God was a natural part of the day. We were friends. We did not run or hide from Him. Since our fall, it takes the utmost discipline to spend time talking with Him. If we are not consistently vigilant, we begin to think He does not love us. Even with the Spirit living in us, there is a constant pressure to sin.

That is why the Lord constantly tells us to not judge on what we see. The truth is usually what we do not see. When we see someone who is physically or mentally challenged, how do we love him or her? By looking past what we see and loving their spirit. How do we do that? The Lord will show us how if we let Him. When you love a person's spirit, you can't help but love everything else about them.

That is not to say God does not want everyone healthy and whole, of course He does. He does not judge us on the effects of sin, neither should we judge people on the effects of sin. He judges us on what our will chooses. That is why He constantly sends trials our way - they are designed to purify our will. It was our will that said yes to sin; it will be our will that says no to sin.

Fear: This is what I call the enemy's unseen weapon. It is very natural for us humans to have various fears about various things in this fallen world. It is very hard to distinguish between when it is us and when it is the enemy, hence, unseen. It took me years to be able to distinguish between the two, and even then, they had to be such unreasonable fears that even I finally caught on.

Fear will paralyze, fear will terrorize, and fear is not logical, reasonable or compassionate. Fear will drive you out of the Body of Christ; fear will keep you away from the Body of Christ. Fear is ugly. The only thing Christians are *supposed* to fear is the Lord. Often the last thing Christians fear, *is* the Lord. Because He is usually the last thing that we fear, we leave ourselves open to fear everything else. As a species, we fear almost everything. As a species, the Lord gave us dominion over everything. Probably, the most common fear for humans is other humans. This is usually the fear that the enemy will use against us.

This fear would probably be neutralized if we gave people more grace. If someone is giving a speech in front of a group of people and they tell a joke that just falls flat as soon as it is uttered, most people in the audience feel bad for the person or they are embarrassed for them. Why? Because if you were up there you would be feeling very embarrassed. We project ourselves. If Person A is used to speaking and telling bad jokes and it does not ruffle Person A, when Person B tells a joke and it falls flat it probably would not matter to Person A.

A person is new to a high school and it is their senior year. Everyone has his or her social circles established. When the person walks into the cafeteria at lunchtime everyone has his or her seat picked out. There is one empty table. If you were a military brat this probably would not faze you because you know it is just a matter of time. If this was a new situation for you and something you have desperately tried to avoid most of your school life, then this is trauma. We project ourselves. The military brat is feeling the same fear only they have learned to control and walk through the fear.

Fear is nothing but the thought of 'the absolute worst that could happen.' If we go to visit the Grand Canyon and we stand on the very edge of the rim we feel fear. Why? Because the worst that could happen is that we could fall off the edge and be killed, and be killed in a painful way! If we can always answer the question of "what is the worst that could happen?" we will begin to master many of our fears.

We fear people, they may not accept us or like us, they may laugh at us, and they may humiliate us. What is the worst that can happen? What if they do not like us? With all the humans on the planet, surely we can find a group of people that think we are all that. Even without other people helping, we will humiliate ourselves – so we need to get over that one anyway. We project ourselves.

Fear will cause the gifts in us to lie dormant. The Lord could have gifted you with a beautiful voice to praise Him in song. Your fear of what other people will think or say has caused that gift to lie dormant. Now in all truth, some people do not have a gift in song and they just need to accept that, but many of us do and we know that the only time that gift comes out is in the shower! Go ahead, backhand that ol' slew-footed liar, throw your head back and let that voice soar!

If you are able to control and walk through your fears, you will make the enemy an unhappy camper. Fear is a lie of presumption. Your mind presumes to know how the future will play out. Bring all of your thoughts into the captivity of your Lord! The Lord constantly says, 'Do not fear.' Beloved, what can separate us? What is the worst that can happen? For those unreasonable fears that are obvious attacks from the enemy we can just say the Name above all names and we will be amazed at how the attack is cut short. It seems that when Jesus comes on the scene the demons flee.

Do not be afraid of sudden fear, nor of the onslaught of the wicked when it comes; for the Lord will be your confidence, and will keep your foot from being caught. Prov.3: 25-26

I do not want you to get the impression that fear is a mind over matter thing. It is not. It is an ugly thing. We need to remember that Jesus conquered that also. Many of my fears I have had to battle in prayer to defeat, often waking up in the middle of the night to spend time in the Word battling various fears. It is a battle with the enemy and ourselves. It is a battle that the Lord says "we are *more than* conquerors." He cannot lie.

Delay: If there is anything that will cramp our style, it has to be waiting. We do not like to wait. We go to a restaurant and it irritates us to wait longer than *we think* is needed. If we are waiting to meet a friend for coffee, Lord help them if they are late. We like things when we like them. It is hard for us to understand that it is not our planet. The enemy knows this - or do you think Daniel was the only one who had a delayed answer to prayer?

When you pray, believe and know that the Lord hears and <u>will</u> answer. He would not command us to pray just so He could *not* pay attention. We are made in His image; His words have power and our words have power. Do not let delay shake your faith. Some people call the Lord slow moving but we all often forget that He did bring the floods, He did destroy Egypt, He did come in the flesh, He did rise again, Israel is in their own country, times are getting darker. If He speaks it, it will be so. Trust Him. If you have to wait, it is for a good reason.

> *I would have despaired had I not believed that I would see the goodness of the Lord in the land of the living. Wait for the Lord. Be strong and let your heart take courage. Yes, wait for the Lord. Ps. 27:14*

The Lord does answer and He does move.

Pride: Well, this is the mother lode. What can I say? When you have everything working for you, this will bring down the house. King David was winning victory after victory. Israel was a blessed nation. God was pleased. Then David probably got hit with a fiery dart (*thought out of nowhere*). "How many men are in <u>my</u> army?" I am sure it was just a random thought. David did what most of us do; he did not quench the dart. The dart just kept working its way deeper. God told David not to number his armies because then he would begin to think that the victories were by his own strength. He would begin to not rely on God.

Well, we all know the story; David counted his army, David got puffed up in his own mind; God had to pop the bubble. Pride will undo you when you are doing well or not so well. The problem with pride is that it is a lie; it is a deception. There are no shifting shadows with our God. *Nor will He have it for His children.*

Pride would have you believe that you exist without God's help, instead of His breath. Pride would have you believe that you pulled yourself up by your own bootstraps, instead of His mercy.

Pride would have you believe that you are a pretty good person, instead of someone that arrogantly shoves God aside. Pride would have you believe that you care more about another human being than the very One that sustains all humans. Pride will utterly distort the picture. It will always have the picture with *you* on the throne.

For those of us with low self-esteem and think that pride is not an issue, don't fool yourself, it's pride. Pride will keep the focus on us and not God, by any means necessary. Most of us with low self-esteem will elevate anyone in our lives except the Lord. Indeed, anybody. Can you understand why the Lord hates pride? It is not the truth; it is a deception that we buy into everyday. Either we think we are on the throne or beneath the throne, either way, it is not the truth.

The definition in the dictionary for pride is, "a sense of one's own self; dignity; self-respect." If we do not acknowledge the One who made us, how can we have a sense of self? Pride would have us believe that we do not need God, we can be equal with God, and we can even be God.

That may sound a bit over the top, but for those of us who are born again, is it? After walking with the Lord a few years, we have a tendency to get very pious. We forget the slime pit the Lord pulled us out of. Even for the Sunday school saints, we pat our backs on the fact that we did not slip into sin *that* deeply. We were all in filthy rags until He clothed us in robes of righteousness. There is none good, no, not one.

We often forget that fact when we serve on the mission board, or find success in teaching, or we are a popular youth pastor, or a dynamic evangelist. We begin to ever so slowly think we are more earnest, more righteous.

We can remember more scripture than our brother next to us, we know the deep things of the Bible better than the rest of our Bible study group, we pray a *prettier* prayer than the sister next to us in our prayer group. If we have someone in our church that just will not mature as fast as we think he or she ought to, suddenly we have a condescending manner towards him or her.

Pride is a cold thing. The embraces we give in pride have no warmth. The husband that is not on the same spiritual level as his wife knows something about cold embraces. The wife that prays for her husband "to just be on fire for Jesus" has no clue that pride is pushing that prayer. How long has the Lord waited for *you* to be "on fire" for Him? Has He ever made you feel that you do not measure up? No, not ever.

If you loved your husband as Christ has and still does love you, your husband would be "on fire." In your pride, you have killed the very thing that you pray for. It applies to either spouse - husbands can flip the script. The enemy is having a good time in too many Christian marriages.

Pride is a vicious thing and the Lord hates it. We may fool everyone, but He lives in our heart, He sees what is there. He is not impressed.

Pride will come in any form imaginable; your car, your house, your kids, your salary, your hair, your looks, your skills, anything - whatever it takes to deceive you into thinking that *you, alone,* did it or can achieve it. Was it not God that formed you and gave you those looks and those skills? Was it not God that gave you that intelligence or the job that followed or the salary that followed or the house that followed or the boat that surely followed that? Was it not God? Pride says it was not God. I did it.

The most arrogant thing that I have heard is, "I believe in a higher being." We will go to any extreme to not bow that knee to the One True God that loves us unconditionally. Obviously this higher being requires nothing of us; we can just go and do as we please. Only humans could come up with that one. But, I digress.

Rebelliousness is pride, which is as the sin of witchcraft. Why? It is a deception. It is willful rebellion against the True God. Witchcraft deceives you into thinking that there is *another* power that will solve your issues. Pride deceives you into thinking *you* can or have solved your issues. Our hatred for God is truly exposed when we walk in rebellion. We will sit on the throne at any cost; sometimes the cost is our soul for eternity. Until we can create something out of nothing, we have nothing to brag about.

Pride would have no place in us if we just accepted ourselves for who we are, vessels of clay. We are no more, no less. The only thing that makes us special is that Jesus lives within. We are not anything beyond that, and yet... that is everything.

Chapter Two

Seriously Buffed Saints

For though we walk in the flesh we do not war according to the flesh. 2 Cor. 10:3

I think if anybody hopes to win a fight they have to identify who or what they are fighting against. I don't know if we as a people, the body of Christ, just don't give this fight much thought or maybe we are in a deep stupor. I do know we have someone pounding on us constantly and we do not really fight back often or intelligently. I don't even think very many of us take spiritual boxing lessons. I don't think many churches have boxing gyms to train saints on how to be prizefighters.

Noah was a seriously buffed saint. Abraham, Isaac and Jacob were seriously buffed saints. Moses, David, Isaiah, Daniel were all seriously buffed saints. Peter, James, John, Paul all were "ripped." Beloved, I think we need to start working out. God has called us to be seriously buffed and we just keep working on those biscuits and gravy.

Bedrock Saints: From Adam to the last human, there had to be, somewhere in that timeline, the "first time" the Lord did something with a human. The brothers & sisters that are mentioned in the Bible are the ones that assisted the Lord in laying the "bedrock" of the message that the Lord wanted to convey to us humans. The message is real simple; the Lord made us, we got ourselves in a mess, the Lord found a way for us to get out of the mess, and if we are wise, we will take it and live forever. Pretty simple for us a stroke of genius on the Lord's part.

They are the "firsts," they are the "bedrock" and the Lord has and will honor them for their willingness and obedience in being a part of His work. I think of people like Enoch, Abraham, Daniel, Jeremiah, Peter, James, John and Paul. They are all giants of the faith, people to emulate and study, friends of God. They were helping the Lord to convey His message.

They are not different from you and I. The Lord made one species of humans. We all have Adam's blood. The Lord is still conveying His message to humans. He would still like people to help convey His message. He would still enjoy having new friends. He does not change. Many of us think the saints in the Bible are the only ones that could go that deep with God. I beg to differ. He is not partial. Nothing holds us back from an intimate walk with Jesus but ourselves. He does not reserve Himself from us.

If you want to part seas, walk where Moses walked. If you want to see the third heaven, drink out of the same cup as Paul. Jesus has put the offer out there; we can be "one with Him and the Father." These brothers and sisters paid a price; they sacrificed something (*everything*) to walk that close to Life. If we are willing, Jesus is willing. We cannot expect to have it easy, the blood that bought us was too precious; we must set our minds for sacrifice and hide our life in Christ.

Ezekiel never talks about it but it is obvious that lying on one side of your body for a year is not the most comfortable way to spend the year. If you want to be buffed, you have to work out in the Lord's gym. Maybe we all do not get to be in the Bible but He is still writing in the books. The saints in the Bible did not get muscled out overnight either. Abraham did not start out as "the father of faith." He started out as Abram. If you read the scriptures carefully, you can see where he stumbled along just like you and I until he slowly started building up those muscles. When he said "ah" that is when the Lord changed his name to Abr*ah*am.

Beloved, you will work up a sweat in the gym, but with time and effort the Lord will help you build those muscles. Most of us want walks like Moses or Paul but you really need to look at their walks and make sure you really count the cost. Abraham wandered most of his life. He did not get to retire and he did not get to buy an RV and roam around the country or take a cruise. Many of these great saints had raised dysfunctional families. It is not all healing the sick and raising the dead; there was a lot of 'behind the scenes' crying out to God.

Peter and Paul never really had a chance to have a nice home with a nice donkey in the garage. Neither one had a pleasant death either. Some of us are called to walks like Jeremiah or Hosea. No one really liked Jeremiah. Hosea had an unfaithful wife. These people are in The Book not because they had *pretty* walks but because, when everything was said and done, they loved and obeyed God. "If you love me, obey my commandments." It is a tough gym, only the committed stay; only the committed get buffed.

Muscle Groups: So if we are going to get built up what do we do and what are we building up? Each of us probably has areas that are looking pretty good and some areas that are looking pretty shabby. In the physical realm when you workout you do not just work out one area you work out the whole body. In the spiritual realm, it is the same.

Faith: We are constantly exhorted to build up our most holy faith and this needs to be done just like we walk everyday. It is a necessity to survive. It will help us to get around to do our various chores. It will enable us to go on various outings that will enhance our lives. It enables us to go to the "store" to get our food to eat. Without faith, it is impossible to please God.

Okay, the first obvious muscle builder would be to believe that God does exist. What is the point of doing anything else if God does not exist? Most Christians believe God exists but few of us *act* like He exists. If we get a little behind in our bills, we seldom look to God for the answer. We may begin to work a few extra hours at work or, the most likely response would be, to begin to worry. We wouldn't worry a lot, just on the edges of our mind. We really believe our pay is coming from our employer, we really believe our pay sustains us. We don't say it but we live like we believe that.

Our employer's health benefits are inadequate for our health needs. We fret, we get angry, we get disappointed, we worry, and we feel vulnerable. If we are God's precious inheritance, why would He abandon us? He is all knowing, He is sovereign and we are the apple of His eye. If our coverage is not adequate, did He not say that His grace is sufficient? He has given His word that He will take care of us and He cannot lie.

So, what do you do when you are at home on the couch in excruciating back pain and your medical coverage does not allow you to see a doctor? You go to your God. What is the point of having a God if you can't go to Him with your ailments? We exercise our faith that He does care for us, that He does have a reason for us having this experience – and it is for our good. Faith is about trust. Trust Him to take care of you; whether by healing or comfort, you must believe that He will do what is best *for you*. That should work up a good sweat.

Another good workout for building up faith will be to understand that you really know nothing. Any soldier who wants to be in the ranks of the great ones first has to show himself teachable to his commanding officer. No one will invest his or her time and effort in training you if you do not show a willingness to learn.

The same thing goes in spiritual things. The Captain is more than willing to make you a top-notch soldier if you are just willing to learn. If you have the attitude that you know nothing (*which is the truth*), your commanding officer can pour into you. If you think that you can learn a *few* things from the Lord, then all you will learn is a few things.

A humble person that believes Jesus is the Captain of the Host will watch His every move. They will watch to see His strategies; they will watch everything about Him. The more you watch the Captain the more you will copy Him. You will find yourself thinking and moving like Him. That is not so bad considering our Captain made a public display of the demons when He defeated them in an awesome masterstroke of warfare. If we are going to learn warfare, we might as well learn from the best. First we have to believe that the Captain has something to teach us and we have something to learn. That is a hard thing to do but it is a necessary thing.

The classic faith builder is to take a promise of God's and just believe it. God cannot lie. Lets take, for instance, Abraham and Sarah. God promised Abraham a son. Abraham was way, way past child producing age and Sarah was way, way, way past child-bearing age. In fact, if God had given that promise to some of us, we would have tossed it off as a whimsical thought. Since Abraham had been working out in the gym, he grabbed it and held on. As he held on, his faith grew stronger and stronger. Wow!! If you step out and believe God, He will strengthen your faith. Whew! Better take a sip of water. Let's go to high burn!

Prayer: Beloved, it is okay to tell God that you do not know how to pray. It is okay to tell your leaders and elders that you do not know how to pray. If you just came from the world of darkness into the world of light, you really have not had an opportunity to learn *how* to pray. Put that pride aside and ask somebody! Most of us watch other people and, after awhile, we imitate them or we read the Lord's Prayer and expand on that. For myself, after years of hit and miss prayers, I just asked the Lord to show me how to pray and pray effectively. He showed me the secret to a 100% guaranteed answer every time, effective prayer life. Would you like to know? Come on work that muscle! Would you really like to know? Okay, it is really pretty simple: pray according to His will or His character or *what He would pray.*

You ask, what does that mean? That means, when you are laughed at or avoided by co-workers for being a Christian, you pray for them. I don't mean that you just mutter, "Lord, bless them." You stop and allow the Lord to give you His thoughts and you pray for them. You pray for them to experience His comfort in their life that you enjoy all the daylong. You pray for them to come to know His love that you wrap yourself in everyday. You pray for them to understand that they need a Savior to rescue them just like you were rescued. Your co-workers are lost, they do not know any better and they are living a life with no hope. If you do not pray for your enemies, who will?

Your teenager refuses to go to church with you and thinks that church has no relevance in their life. What do you do? You pray with the mind of Christ. Before you nag or threaten them for the hundredth time to come to church with you, before you even ask them, you go to your Counselor. He is the One who saves, not you. Parents often make the mistake of thinking that they love their kids more than the Lord does. It is by the Lord's wooing (*drawing*) that your child will come to a saving knowledge of Christ anyway. Why not go to the Captain and get the strategy of how to win your child for Him? Feel the burn, oh yeah.

And when you do pray, go in your room and shut the door. There is no need to let the rest of the family know when we pray. If we are sincerely praying, they will know. There is no need to let the congregation know that we get up before the sunrise to pray. What is the purpose? What we do in secret the Lord will reward us openly. That is the power of prayer. The more we pray, the more time we spend with the Lord. The more time we spend with the Lord, the more we become like Him. Hmm, is there a connection here? After awhile, we will discover a wonderful thing. The Lord is enjoyable to get to know. It is delightful to spend time with Him. I know that is hard to comprehend.

The Lord's gym is for the committed, I didn't say it wasn't fun to hang out there. Why do you think people are willing to die for Him?

Hope: Okay, this is the muscle that gets worked out no matter what; it would be like our lungs or heart. If they aren't working, we aren't working. For humans, if hope is not working, we are not working. Whether you are saved or not, you will exercise hope. It is just what we do. When we are in the Kingdom we must train ourselves to hope in Kingdom things. We cannot put our hope in the lottery ticket to solve our financial issues. We cannot put our hope in the company we work for to take care of us in our old age. We cannot put our hope in the medical field to cure us of our life threatening illness. I know that is an easy thing to write, especially if you are looking into the eyes of your child who is fevered and has clammy skin and has lost consciousness and the doctor says that there is nothing else that can be done, what do you do? Most humans will usually, without thinking instinctively cry out to God. It is what we do. When you strip everything away, our pretensions, our assumptions, our arrogance we find out that we know exactly in Who to put our hope. He blesses the righteous and the unrighteous. But there is more.

Living a life without hope of something better is like living in a murky shadow world with no color. People, we can live a life beyond the saving up for the 401K, without the stress of Social Security being there when we retire, without the ugly realization that having the most toys does not mean you win. There is more to life than what we know. There is a life free from fear, free from being intimidated, free from the anxiety of not being accepted. There is a place where everything *is* right and good. There is a place where everyone loves everyone else. There is a place where there is no poor or sick or dying. There is a place where we can be whole. We were not put here to do our 90 years the best we can and then die. There is absolutely more.

We instinctively hope for it. When we see the starving kids on the TV commercials, something in us longs for a better planet. That prick we feel deep in our soul is from God. He tries to tell us everyday of our lives that there is something better that He has planned for us, but we shut out His voice before He is even done speaking. For those of us with the knowledge that we are passing through, we often hope - but we don't hope with the mind of Christ. We hope for the sweet bye and bye not realizing that the Kingdom is within us. We can have that abundant, rich life now, here. I am not saying that anything is wrong with hoping for the City not made with hands. Many a time, that is all that will get you through some trials.

If the enemy can steal our hope, he will destroy us. Without hope the people perish. Our hope must be in Jesus. He is the resurrection. He is the bright Morning Star. He is the Alpha and the Omega. Heaven would be lonely without Him. Who else do we know? That is what Jesus was trying to get across to Mary and Martha, don't hope in the sweet bye and bye, hope in Him. He is the Hope of Glory! We carry that Hope within us. That is the awesomeness of the resurrection, the Hope lives and He lives within us. When life gets too heavy for you to go on, look within, not to yourself, you don't need some self-help philosophy. None of us needs a feel good god. None of us needs a religion or some creed to adhere to. We need a God that is real. A God that is alive. A God that will save us, counsel us, guide us, and lead us. We need the real deal. There is only one God. He is our hope. He will give us life and He will add the color and substance to our life. He will add the rich textures and nuances and wonders to our life. That is what we need, that is what we really hope for. We hope for the One True Living God and, for those of us in the Kingdom, He is within.

We have to learn to draw on the Hope within to get through life or we will miss the Life within. Okay, lets go for the cool down.

Love: How do you love someone who is putting a big nail through your hands? How do you love someone who has just dipped you in boiling oil? How do you love someone who has just killed your best friend? How do you love a co-worker who can't stand the sight of you? How do you love a boss that is committed to getting you fired? The same way you love your child that has not spoken to you in fifteen years. You love them anyway. How does God love us? If He does not transform us, we can't stand Him. Come on let's get truthful. Before we got saved, God was the last thing in our thoughts. We could care less if we hurt Him or not. Most of us preferred if He just stayed out of our way. He loved us anyway. This love thing that we experience with God did not just start when we were finally able to accept His love, He loved us while we were in our sins.

God wants us to show that same love to other people. He doesn't want us to love them after they are cleaned up and able to love us back, that would not be like Him. He wants us to love people before they are able to love us back, if they are *ever* able to love us back. The problem with that is that we are not able to love like that. We are only able to give what has been given. The closest we come to loving like God is with our children. They are unable to love us back when they are babies and we love them anyway. But would we if they weren't cute and cuddly and so obviously helpless? Probably not. We love because He first loved us.

Real love has nothing to do with what we are or what we will receive back. Real love has nothing to do with the emotion that we feel for a person. Real love is saying that we will stick by this person. We stick by them because we said we would. Jesus said, "If you love me, obey my commandments." If we want to show Jesus that we love Him, we will obey His commandments. That has nothing to do with warm and fuzzy feelings. You either obey or you don't. If you want to love God more, you just have to be more obedient. But what does love have to do with spiritual warfare? Everything. If you love your enemy (*not **the** enemy*), they can't comprehend it and you will send satan into a tizzy.

It is so beyond us to love our enemies that we will have to go to God to do this. How did Daniel grow up in Babylon and love his captors? I am sure he needed to pray three times a day. How does Paul, after being stoned in Lystra, go back into the city to continue preaching to the same people? That is a love that the enemy can't defeat. That is how the Lord wants us to be, not to walk as *mere* men. Anyone can love a friend, but to love an enemy is a divine thing, it is to be like Jesus.

You say, "well that's nice but how do I get there?" Just like every other saint before you, you go to the Lord and ask to be changed. There is no shortcut. It will eventually lead you to the cross. You will have to die to doing things your way and just trust that God will take care of you. If you love your enemies in obedience to God, He will set a table before you in the presence of your enemies. He promised it, He cannot lie. Go ahead, die and let

Jesus show you what it means to be like Him. It is not the warm, fuzzy love, it is the real thing and you will probably be quite surprised at what it looks like.

If you do this workout everyday, you are guaranteed to turn into a seriously buffed saint. All the saints that you read about had to go to this gym and they definitely went through this workout. The rest is left up to your determination but you can be assured that the buffed saints are surrounding you and cheering you on!

Chapter Three

The Big Bad Wolf and Company

For our struggle is not against flesh and blood, but against the rulers, against the powers, against the world forces of this darkness, against the spiritual darkness, against the spiritual forces of wickedness in the heavenly places. Eph. 6:12

Everything was made by, for and through God. God created everything. God created power. God created all authorities. God created the principalities. God created the forces. God created the rulers. Everything God created was good.

Lucifer was cast out of Heaven and he took a third of the angels with him. He was the worship leader in heaven; he had a lot of influence. When he came down to Earth, he was mad and so were his friends. They lost their bid for power and they lost the glory that they had. They hate humans. Whether we are looking for them or not, they will be looking for us to make our life miserable and to eventually destroy us.

The Kingdom of Heaven suffers violence. There is rebellion in God's creation. We have to understand this. There are spiritual forces of wickedness <u>in the heavenly places</u>. Many Christians really don't give much thought to 'spiritual forces of wickedness.' We know it has something to do with satan and it is real bad but we don't really give it much contemplation. Because of this, we are usually in a reactionary mode instead of an offensive mode when we come up against these powers. You may say to yourself that you will just mind your own business and try to be good and you won't have to deal with these issues. That is what pastors are for, anyway. Unfortunately, you are interacting with these powers everyday.

If satan is the ruler of this world and there is a big powerful corporation in this world, where do you think they get their power? I am not saying every big corporation is evil. I am saying that there are only two powers in the universe, light and dark. If you are not serving the Light, then you are serving darkness. Maybe not intentionally, but doing something in ignorance does not make it right or good. There are powers that are strategically manipulating the human race. The manipulation comes in all kinds of forms whether it is sexual, good works, the pursuit of adventure, the pursuit of self, the pursuit of fame, the pursuit of knowledge, intellectual pride (the new "geek is cool" trend) or just good ol' fashioned ambition. Whatever it takes to keep you occupied, away from Jesus, until your last breath is what will be used.

Take for instance the Third Reich. The Third Reich could not have gotten as far as it did without some spiritual power in back of it giving it its power and influence. On this planet, there are principalities and powers in back of many of the institutions and organizations that are used for commerce, education, entertainment, religion and government. Everything must happen in the spiritual world first and then we see the trickle down effect in the physical world.

The Lord tells us that our battle is not with flesh and blood but with the spiritual powers manipulating that person or institution. There was a period of time when well-meaning Christians were going around bombing abortion clinics. At the time this was happening, I knew that they did not understand that their fight was in the spiritual realm. We cannot defeat a spiritual power with a physical bomb. But you can believe that the spiritual power behind abortion was enjoying each and every bombing. The enemy is not stupid, he has been around humans since we were first created and he knows what strings to pull to move the masses or the individual.

If we want to fight an unjust government or an unjust company we have to go to prayer and ask the Lord to show us the power or spiritual force in back of the organization. When the Lord does reveal the power or authority, we need to wait and get our strategy for attack. We cannot just run out with our Bible and think we will defeat it. It is a power, an authority, and we are human. Fortunately for us Christians the Lord has given to us (*His body*) the gift of discernment. There are brothers and sisters that can discern the various spirits moving in and around people and organizations.

Remember in the book of Acts when Paul had a lady following him around declaring that he was doing the works of God? What the lady was saying sounded okay on the surface; it was only through spiritual discernment that Paul perceived that she was really not glorifying God. Remember, the Third Reich had the backing of the German Church for most of its time in power. <u>We will need discernment</u>.

> *And no wonder, for even satan disguises himself as an angel of light. Therefore it is not surprising if his servants also disguise themselves as servants of righteousness, whose end shall be according to their deeds. 2 Cor.11: 14-15*

If evil was not successful at being deceptive, we would not be in the situation we are.

I think of the time before the Reformation, it was a dark time for the Church. The Church *did not know* it was in a dark time. The principalities are clever beings, but greater is He that is in you than he that is in the world. In this day and age, the Church has its work cut out for it. If you want to know what powers to fight against, just look around and see what people are worshiping: Money, Sex, Self (*Humanism*), Fun (*Hedonism*), Gluttony, Self, Intellectualism (*Elitism*), Military Might (*War*), Self, Technology with a capital T, and Religion. There are others, of course, but this will give you a good start.

Self is in there a few times because, in truth, self motivates almost everything we do.

> *But realize this that in the last days difficult times will come. For men will be lovers of self, lovers of money, boastful, arrogant, revilers, disobedient to parents, ungrateful, unholy, unloving, irreconcilable, malicious gossips, without self-control, brutal, haters of good, treacherous, reckless, conceited, lovers of pleasure rather than lovers of God; holding to a form of godliness, although they have denied its power... always learning and never able to come to the knowledge of the truth. 2 Tim.3: 1-7*

We buy the car so we can look good. We buy the house so people can see that we are successful. We buy the fashionable clothes so people will think we are "with it." We save our money to take our trips so we can enjoy ourselves, after all "we deserve it." We buy the latest RV so we can look good pulling into the RV Park. Christians are very much included.

Lets talk about church. If the pastor and his wife don't specifically say "hi" to us, we have a bad day. If they do say "hi" to us, we think we are special because they spoke to us. Most of our prayers concern us. We ask God if He could do this for us or would He deliver us from that. Me, me, me. Our anxieties with our walk usually concern "am *I* really saved?" I could go on and on but I think you get the point. Most of our life is concerned with our self. Trust me, I'm talking about myself, also. Most of this concern is natural to humans but the dark spiritual powers definitely exploit and take advantage of the situation.

We have to understand that the God we talk to on a daily basis is not our private God; He is the God of the nations also. If we can take our eyes off of our problems for a moment, we would realize that there is a bloody, soul-destroying war going on and the enemy we are fighting is not to be played with or ignored. While we sit around throwing our temper tantrums or having a pity party, there are saints out there dying for the Gospel. God is ministering to people all over the world. Saints are crying out to Him for food because there is nothing left to eat *in the country*. They are beseeching God for antibiotics so their child will not die from infection as they lie in a filthy makeshift hospital. They are believing God to bring peace in a war torn country instead of a new Cadillac in the driveway; God is showing Himself mighty on behalf of saints around the world. He is just waiting for us to join the fight.

Our life will never be pain-free; the Garden of Eden is closed for now. The only peace and joy we will find will be when we are doing God's will for our lives. My brothers and sisters, we just have to grow up. We have to accept our responsibility as citizens of the Kingdom. That means we ask God for wisdom and discernment about this spiritual war that is going on around us. It is real - you are either fighting or you are a casualty. Our pastors should not be the only ones on the front lines. We all should be there. We all should be studying the Word to bring a good word to the saints; we all should be going about visiting the sick, the elderly and the imprisoned. We all should be concerned about the orphans and the widows. The enemy has lulled us to sleep and we need to wake up! It is not about us, it is not our show. We just have a bit part in God's show. Some of us have a small speaking part, but we are not the stars. He is.

The enemy is good at distracting us. Instead of getting a bigger house, maybe we could support a missionary with our extra funds. Instead of getting the latest model car, maybe we could send some money to an organization that is helping to feed the poor. Instead of going out to dinner with our friends, maybe *once in awhile* we could hold a prayer meeting with our friends and pray for the saints that are being persecuted. Ask the Lord what He would have you do. The work is there the workers are few. <u>Please do not misunderstand me.</u> It is not that the Lord does not want to bless us with these things. These things are wonderful and fun. We have to remember, we are in a war, and we are passing through. Some of us may get blessed with the wealth of this world and that is great. I am saying, let's not put more effort into that than we do into seeking God. We can have our pleasures later; let's roll up our sleeves and get to work.

Some of us may think that we have an option as to how intense our walk needs to be. We really don't. We all should know the Bible as well as any biblical scholar. We all should be serving as diligently as any missionary. We all should be walking the deeper realms of prayer. This is a battle for our soul and where our soul will be for eternity; there is nothing more important than that. It is so important that God became flesh and suffered to *make* a way for us to live forever. The enemy has a goal, and a strategy to achieve it. His goal is to take as many of God's creatures with him to Hell. The enemy knows that God loves us. The enemy knows that each soul that he is able to keep from the Savior agonizes

God's heart. The enemy is jealous and obviously has serious esteem issues.

If the enemy can deceive us into thinking we are a good person without need of a savior - that is fine with him. If the enemy can deceive us into thinking that if we serve him (*satanist, occult*) we will be rewarded - that is fine with him. If the enemy can deceive us into thinking that allah, buddha or a spirit guide is the god that we should be serving, that is fine with him. If the enemy can deceive us into thinking that God is just focused on a certain race of people - that is fine with him. If the enemy can deceive us into thinking that help for the human race will come from the cosmos - that is fine with him. The enemy will use any and all means necessary to keep us distracted from the Truth. The enemy is playing for keeps.

The enemy will use finances to keep us distracted. Whether it is an abundance of funds or the lack of funds, it is all the same to him because it achieves the same ends. For those of us who are workaholics, our employer may enjoy that trait in us but it is deadly to our marriage and family. For those of us in full-time ministry the enemy enjoys keeping us focused on "the work of the Kingdom" while our marriage and family get torn apart. We have to remember which Kingdom we are trying to further. If we cannot show our own household Christ in us, we are not furthering the Kingdom of God. We have to remember that we are behind enemy lines with a particularly vicious enemy who knows almost all of our weak points.

In order that no advantage be taken of us by satan; for we are not ignorant of his schemes. 2 Cor. 2:11

Beloved, the enemy is not above using fear to keep our mouth closed. The less we talk about our Savior, the better. The enemy is not above using peer pressure to make us feel that we are the odd ones for believing in Jesus. We must see these things for what they are. If we started speaking to people about Jesus more people would be snatched out of the enemy's hands. That is why the Christians that preach the Gospel usually suffer the worst persecutions. They do not fear the worldly powers they only fear the One. They are also the ones that are rewarded with the intimate walks. If he can keep us distracted fighting about speaking in tongues, whether to sprinkle or immerse, whether God is coming pre, mid or post tribulation he will use any and all means to keep us from our primary duty which is to preach the Good News.

Beloved, remember Desert Storm. Hussein knew he lost the war and as his troops retreated they blew up the oilrigs and destroyed towns along the way. The enemy is the same way, he knows he can't win the war but he is going for maximum desolation and devastation in the meantime.

War is not fun, but sometimes we must fight to have peace. Saints, this is one of those times. We must fight, the Captain has assured us of victory; we must take courage and go right up to the gates of hell and never retreat - only advance.

Chapter Four

The Captain and Company

Bless the Lord, all you His hosts, you who serve Him, doing His will. Ps. 103:21

I think the first thing we who are in the body of Christ need to understand is that this is not our war. This war started before we were created. Since we were the last ones to enter the war, it would probably be wise on our part to find out what is going on. The best way to do that is to sit in on the briefings that the Captain gives everyday. As I have explained earlier, this may not be our war but the enemy is definitely targeting us. We all know Jesus as Savior, as Lord, as our Friend, but maybe we do not realize that He is also a warrior. The definition of the word captain is: "a subordinate officer commanding under a sovereign or general." I think we all know Who the sovereign general is. Jesus is the Captain of the Lord's army, He is familiar with war, and He has already defeated the enemy.

Who are the Lord's hosts? They are His creation. The sun, moon, planets, stars, the creatures around the throne, the angels in heaven and all of the other beings in heaven that we know nothing about; and they all find pleasure in doing the Lord's will. The hosts are also the saints that have gone before us. The Lord has a big entourage and He would like us to join. The Captain will never hesitate to use all of His hosts to assure us of a victory. Remember when Joshua asked the Lord to hold the sun? Everything in creation serves His purposes, whether willingly or unwillingly, that is why He is the Sovereign Lord. The war is won. So, what exactly are we battling and what is He, the Captain, leading us in?

Yes, the war is won, death is defeated, we have eternal life, the enemy will be cast into the lake of fire BUT we do not believe that. That is what the Lord battles everyday. The enemy is the father of lies and he constantly lies to us *and we believe him.* We also help the enemy along with our sinful nature; we naturally pull away from the things of God.

When you look back in the Old Testament (*yes, we have to go there*), the Lord gave the Israelites the Promised Land. We know the Lord cannot lie. If God promised it, we know that is better than gold in the bank. So, why did the Israelites have to spy out the land? They could have walked into the land at midnight with no weapons and the residents would have had to leave. The Lord promised them that they would eat of fruit that they did not plant and fields that they did not sow and live in houses that they did not build!

As they spread out into this new territory one scripture keeps repeating itself. It repeats so often it gets sort of embarrassing. In the book of Judges it says, "but Manasseh did not take possession of...' 'But they did not drive them out completely.' 'Neither did Ephraim drive out.' 'Zebulun did not drive out.' 'Asher did not drive out.' 'Naphtali did not drive out...' One absolutely shocking scripture pops out that continues to stun me:

> *'Then the Amorites <u>forced</u> the sons of Dan into the hill country, for they did not <u>allow</u> them to come down to the valley. Judges 1:34*

The sons of Dan had the promise, they did not believe. We know the Old Testament was given to us to be a tutor. And even though we can read these scriptures and see very clearly the mistakes that our forefathers made, we seldom learn the lesson. We often live the lives of the tribe of Manasseh or Naphtali and often the tribe of Dan.

The Lord in His great mercy still allows us to live in the land with a semblance of conquest but He desires a higher road for us. Take a look at this:

> *Now the angel of the Lord came up from Gilgal to Bochim. And he said, 'I brought you up out of Egypt and led you into the land which I have sworn to your fathers; and I said, 'I will never break My covenant with you, and as for you, you shall make no covenant with the inhabitants of this land; you shall tear down their altars.' But you have not obeyed Me; what is this you have done? "Therefore I also said, 'I will not drive them out before you; but they shall become as thorns in your sides, and their gods shall be a snare to you.'"*
> *Judges 2:1-3*

How many times have we been promised something by the Lord and it is such a phenomenal promise that we don't believe the whole promise? We seldom believe that we are dealing with a God that can do anything and He delights in doing the impossible. I think that is why the Lord takes such pleasure in those few saints that come along and they believe whatever the Lord says, no matter how preposterous it sounds. Enoch was that kind of saint, the Lord couldn't even wait for Enoch to die He just snatched him up!

As you can see from the above scriptures, the Lord wonders why we don't believe Him, also. How many times has something or someone we should have conquered or driven out become a thorn in our side? The Captain has said that we only need a mustard seed of faith to move mountains. Often, His strategy is downscaled to our unbelief. If you look at Moses, the Lord was willing to send *just* Moses - but Moses did not have that kind of faith, *yet*. So, the Lord sent Aaron to be a mouthpiece for Moses.

The Lord is with us always but, if you notice, the Captain would not lead the Israelites until they were baptized and circumcised. The Lord is always with us but the Lord will not lead us until we are set apart. There are those of us who do what we want to do and we try to take the Promised Land on our own; it does not work like that. He will save us but, to get the daily briefings, to be able to drive out the enemy, it takes faith and we have to be set apart. If you think about it, that is just good strategy. If we have not set ourselves apart for the Lord's use *exclusively,* the enemy could have us jumping all over the map. This is very serious business. Souls are being won and lost while we continue to sip our lukewarm soup.

We so often play catch up - the cloud has moved, what was fire is now ashes and we don't perceive it. We spend most of our walk looking back at the glory days of our first taste of the King not realizing it just gets better the longer we walk with Him. Every saint in the Bible increased from glory to glory the longer they walked with the Lord.

I was recently at a church service where the pastor was explaining different ways to worship the Lord. He was saying that we could sing to the Lord and he asked us to follow his example. Everyone sang a short line or two. He said that we could clap to the Lord. Everyone clapped. This went on for raising hands, stomping feet and so on. When he came to prostrating ourselves before the Lord, the pastor gave an example and maybe 20 people out of 1000 followed the example. What is the point of dressing up, driving to church and sitting there for a couple of hours if not to worship the Lord? We have no clue Who we serve.

What if the President of the United States flew to a third world country and found a boy there that had never been outside of his village? He did not have a TV or even a radio, he could only wash in the river and he seldom knew if he was going to get another meal. What if the President told this boy that if he would come with him, he would have three meals a day, a hot shower every day, and he could have a change of clothes every day. Now, we know that is how we live everyday and it is no big deal. But to that boy, he cannot even comprehend that; he would think the President was telling a joke. That is how we are with the Lord. The angels know how true everything is that the Lord promised, they know how magnificent and awesome He is, but we just can't comprehend it.

Often, most often, a situation will come up and we just react. We think we know what the situation is and, instead of consulting with the Captain, we just step in front of Him and usually fall flat on our faces. Remember in the book of Joshua when the Gibeonites deceived the Israelites? Joshua and his leadership team were absolutely sure they knew what was going on. They had no need to ask the Lord for counsel. Well, we all know what happened - they were deceived and they had to honor the promise that they made to the Gibeonites for generations. As I can personally testify, the consequences for not consulting the Captain can be very long term.

We can continue going around in circles or we can get with the program. The enemy knows that there is a war going on. The Captain and His hosts know that there is a war going on. We seem to be the only part of His creation that is just not getting it.

D.M. Carthern

I think about King Josiah; when the Law of the Lord was found and it was read to him, he understood the height from which he and his people had fallen. He understood that repentance was in order and he did not take for granted that mercy would be shown. We need to have that same attitude. When we hear the Word from the Captain, we just need to obey – and quickly. King Josiah could not move quickly enough to put everything back in order. Idols were torn down, false priests were kicked out, and the temple was restored. He was moving with a holy fear. Beloved, we need to pray that whatever gripped his heart, grips our heart. Repentance is a gift - it is not a given fact. God is to be feared, He is the One that can cast our soul into the lake of fire.

Beloved, we need to understand that the Lord's ways are really not our ways. If you look at the Bible and how the Lord has chosen to get His message out it really is not how most of us would choose to get a message out. We would not choose the least popular group of people. Look at our TV commercials; we only pick the beautiful and the popular to represent a product. We would not have our representatives so obviously inadequate for the task. Moses was a Jewish/Egyptian murderer in exile. Moses would have never even been given an interview for a commercial. David was a young sheepherder, not likely to be discovered by Wall Street. Solomon was the wisest man who ever lived, but he was also a promiscuous adulterer and ladies man. Daniel was a slave not likely to grow up to be a leader. The "glorious new covenant" really did not change tactics. John the Baptist wandered out in the desert eating insects with some honey. The first disciples were *just* fishermen. Matthew worked for the IRS. I mean really, if you want to promote something besides Old Spice shaving lotion, most of us would not pick any of these people.

And yet, these are the ones the Lord handpicked and the message they carried is the most enduring message in the history of humankind. Maybe the Lord does know something that we don't. Hmmm, is it possible that it has nothing to do with the messenger? If we are dealing with God, He says that He raises up whomever He wills. He also says He brings down whomever He wills. God is gracious enough to allow us into His adventure. If God can take a murderer and have his name exalted through the ages, think what He could do with the rest of us.

The Captain does have a strategy if we will just stop and listen. He knows how to defeat the enemy in our lives. He knows how to bring us into the fullness of His desires for us. We need to believe and trust Him. **We need to obey Him.** If you notice in the Joshua passage about Jericho, the Captain is very specific on how to defeat Jericho. He does not change. If we go to Him and listen, He is very specific today on how to defeat the enemy in various areas of our lives. How many times have we gone off on our own and made a mess of things? Even for those times that we have gone off and made successes of ourselves as far as the world is concerned, if we can't do the one thing we were made to do, which is to please God, what have we really accomplished? He uses different means to accomplish so much more than we can think of; He is able to think outside of the box. Could it be because He is outside of the box? It sounds so trite, but I think it is true we just need to trust and obey.

The Lord, our Friend, our Captain does not change. He has set His face to have a people, a people that love righteousness and truth, and a people that will love Him from their hearts. He will stop at nothing to see that accomplished. It should be said of us that we are a people with a magnificent obsession, serving the only One who is worthy of all of our strength, mind, heart and soul. We follow so many other things not worthy of our time or talents and when we finally have something that is worth everything we have, we begin to be wishy-washy. This is the time to set our faces like flint; to set aside the earthly weights and just follow our Captain.

We don't need to spy out the land; we don't need to taste the fruit. Like our brothers and sisters before us, we just need to march forward in sober understanding that our Captain has already won the battle and we just need to believe Him. We do not want to be a people that did not drive out our enemies. Let's take the land and hold it until He comes.

So, now that we are pumped up to follow the Captain and we understand the necessity for doing so, what do we do when He leads us into pain? I am talking about those trials that reach deep down into those places that we have not looked at in years. And what do we do when we are in the midst of this pain and we have quoted to ourselves all of the victory scriptures, all of the comfort scriptures, all of the scriptures that tell us that God has a plan for our lives; what do we do when the excruciating pain is still there? The trial just keeps going on? We are sure we cannot bear anymore and we do not see the end in sight? Is this just a way of life from here on out? Will all of our joy from this moment on be a "sacrifice of praise?"

We longingly look at our other brothers and sisters and envy their lightheartedness. Sometimes we stand on the edge of madness because it is never ending. What is the Captain doing? We know we would never walk away but, come on, where is the abundant life? Where are the rivers of living water flowing from our bellies? Where is the blessed life and blessings pressed down, shaken together and running over?

Dear Beloved, I wish we were a different type of people. I wish that once the Lord told us something that we would be quick to believe and obey. I wish that we always ran after the Lord with *all* of our hearts. We all know the truth, though; when we are in pain, we seek the Lord with a focus and an intensity that is not there any other time. When we are in pain and we go to the Lord, our defenses are down; we have all the time in the world to spend with Him. We are there to listen and we really take huge steps in our walks with God. The truth is 'before we were afflicted we went astray.'

> *For Thou hast tried us, O God; Thou hast refined us as silver is refined. Thou didst bring us into the net; Thou didst lay an oppressive burden upon our loins. Thou didst make men ride over our heads; We went through fire and through water; Yet Thou didst bring us out into a place of abundance. Ps. 66:10-12*

For now, the only thing I can say is that when, not if, the Captain leads you into pain, He will also lead you out of pain.

Take a look at Joseph in the Old Testament. He was diligently serving God in the house of Potiphar. He rises quickly because He keeps his eyes on the Lord. In due season, he is in charge of the whole house. I am sure his times in prayer consisted of a lot of praise. God was exalting him in the midst of his captivity. Out of the blue, he gets charged with rape and gets put in prison. The Bible does not speak on this, but we know that Joseph was human just like us. There was no reason at all that Joseph should have been put in prison. He did nothing wrong! He knew it, God knew it and Potiphar's wife knew it. I am sure his first few days in prison he thought it would all work out. Day after day, month after month, you know Joseph went to God many a time asking him when this trial was going to end. Since he is just like us, you know the man was in pain.

He did not know he was going to end up second in command of Egypt. Right then, all he knew was that he was on the fast track to success and the next minute, he was in prison. Yes, he did get to be trustee of the prison, and that is nice, but you know he would rather have just been set free. As soon as he found out that the baker and cupbearer were going to be released, he petitioned them to bring his case before Pharaoh. When those men were released, they did not remember Joseph before Pharaoh. Don't think for a minute Joseph did not take that disappointment to prayer when he finally admitted to himself that both of those guys did not remember him. This was a man that had to walk through a very painful trial - for two more years!

Only when he was at the absolute end of himself did God deliver him. God does not change. We often read the Bible not understanding that these were men and women just like us. Job was blessed at the end of his trial, yes, but I don't know any man that can watch the death of his whole family and not grieve deeply for a long time. Yes, they were replaced, but do you really think Job forgot about them?

What about when the Captain leads us into risky ventures? Of course it is never a risk for Him, but we perceive it as a risk to ourselves. It could cause us to *suffer* loss or injury of something dear to us. W*e* Christians that have been so blessed to live in the United States, give God such a hard time when He tries to move us out of our comfort zone. We seldom sacrifice our time for anyone else. We are so often caught up in our own lives. It usually takes a major move of God to get us to share the Word with our co-workers much less someone in another town or country.

There was a time when saints longed to be sent to other countries; now we fear that the Captain may call us to another country. We forget that the One we serve is the God of the nations. Is it possible that your particular gift is needed somewhere else? Are you open to the Captain sending you to any part of the battlefield? Is He Lord and Captain in sentiment only? I understand the hesitation if you are trying to raise a family, but then on the other hand, God gave you the children, certainly He would not send them in harm's way, right? Or do you think you know how to do things better than God?

Our comfort and security must come from God alone. How can we trust an employer more than we trust our God? How can we trust the stock market more than we trust our God? Has He not promised to take care of us? Don't we know that He keeps all of His promises? Has an employer ever promised that? Has Wall Street? I know it is hard to step out not knowing anything but that the Lord called you to something. I just ask you, do you really think Abram had any less of a concern than you?

Beloved, this is the walk, 'in this world you will have much tribulation.' God does not lie. But be of good cheer, the Captain has overcome the world. The Captain does not lie.

D.M. Carthern

Chapter Five

Strategy to Win

I will instruct you and teach you in the way which you should go; I will counsel you with My eye upon you. Ps.32: 8

It's Monday, the first day of the workweek. You are Manager of Operations at a medical clinic. UPS delivers some critical medicine to your intake facility. It has to be kept at a very cool temperature. One of your staff members receives the package and they diligently deliver it to the doctor that ordered it. The doctor is very busy and they do not get around to opening it until a couple of hours later. They call you and leave you a voice mail that the medicine that they received is the wrong medicine. You do not check your voice mail for another hour. You send one of your staff over to pick up the package and you check the package against the order invoice. It is correct. You call the doctor back and confirm by voice the order number that they want. It is correct. You call the pharmaceutical company and check the invoice number - it is correct.

After intense investigation, you find out that the doctor left out one digit on the order form. You order the correct medicine. In the meantime, the medicine that was shipped is now ruined and the clinic will have to pay for the incorrect medicine. It is expensive medicine. The rest of the order is expected that afternoon from UPS. You specifically order your staff to refuse the order. The order comes. They forget everything and accept the order. Not only that, they open the package to fit all of the medication in the refrigerator. There is no hope of you returning this medicine. The clinic will have to pay for it.

Pause.

At this point your mind is moving at 100mph and your adrenaline is pumping and all you can think about is that someone is going to feel your wrath. There is not any logic behind this response. It is a very normal human response when an obstacle has placed itself in our path. In the swirl of this wind it is very hard to hear the voice of the Spirit.

Resume Play.

You find out which staff member received the package and you shift into overdrive. This is the same youngster that has no vision or motivation for his life. He is always finding a way to be a slacker. He wants to be a policeman someday, but he has put no effort towards achieving that vocation.

Pause.

This is also the same youngster that you have been witnessing to about the love of Jesus and His kingdom. Unknown to you, there is a fierce spiritual battle going on right then. The enemy is waiting to whisper into this youngster's mind negative things about Christians. The Spirit is trying to make you hear His voice.

Resume Play.

You unleash your anger. Oh my, it is an awesome thing. The youngster wilts before the tirade. In your anger you also mention another staff member's name, who just happens to overhear the tirade. After you have vented and your employee is sufficiently instructed and cowed, you go on with your gray Monday. Where is the coffee?

A little while later, after you have had your two cups of java, the employee that you mentioned in your tirade approaches you and says that they were offended that you could not come to them with your dissatisfaction but that you shared it with "everybody."

Pause.

At this point, you could unleash your anger again. You could dismiss them and pay them no mind. Or, you could choose the path of your Lord, which is humility.

Resume Play.

You look at your employee, you allow the Spirit to touch your heart and you apologize and ask their forgiveness.

Unknown to you, you have won a spiritual victory. Yes, it would have been better to vent your anger in a more constructive way. But, when we are presented with a choice to harden our heart or choose humility, it is always better to choose to humble ourselves. The Lord gets tremendous mileage out of that. Most spiritual battles are just like that. They are very daily. It is those little choices that determine how much ground we gain or lose. Most people expect big dramatic battles, and sometimes they are. Most times the battle is in our day-to-day life. How we choose to live our minutes often determines how our life plays out.

The youngster that was being witnessed to now gets a front row seat to view Christian life at its essence. They see the back and forth interactions of us with our Lord, the ups and downs. They see the choices that a Christian must make, the struggles, and the sweet forgiveness. We are not perfect. An unbeliever needs to see that they do not have to be clean before they get in the bathtub.

Beloved, this is the battle, what we do day-to-day determines victories and losses. The Spirit deals with us by the minute, not by the week or by the month. The minutes we spend, or do not spend, with the Lord at the beginning of the day often determine victory or loss.

So what are we trying to win? If the Lord already has the victory, what is the point? What race are we trying to win?

We are trying to win our humanity back.

It really has not registered with us how far we have fallen. When I read the first few chapters of Genesis, I can't help but get an almost overwhelming sadness reading about our first parents. Each time in my mind I keep saying to Eve, "don't eat it don't eat it!" The sadness comes from knowing that she did eat it and of the terrible loss that followed. When I read the scripture of the Lord walking through the Garden during the cool of the day, my heart aches at what was lost. The scripture reads:

> *And they heard the sound of the Lord God walking in the garden in the cool of the day, and the man and his wife hid themselves from the presence of the Lord God among the trees of the garden. Gen.3:8*

They hid themselves from their Maker. The justification that followed is even more tragic. It must have ripped Eve's heart to hear Adam say, "The woman that *You* gave me..." He had earlier professed to God that she was flesh of his flesh. Eve quickly scrambles to pass the blame and the only thing she can think of is to blame a snake. Now, really. It was satan using the snake but I can't believe Eve is trying to blame an animal for her actions. The Fall's consequences were immediate and devastating. The question that was asked by our Maker, we are still trying to answer, "Where are you?" Where are we?

We spend our lives trying to answer that question. What are we doing here? Why do we exist? We look for the answers everywhere - in our parent's eyes, in our friend's eyes, in our spouse's eyes, in our children's eyes and often in our employer's eyes. We look into his or her eyes for confirmation that we are somebody; that we are a person of purpose; that we matter. Even when we do get a confirmation back, we find out that it does not satisfy. Some of us seek the confirmation in fame, some of us seek it in commercial success, and some of us seek it in drugs, sex or various pleasures. The only confirmation that can satisfy is the one that we receive from our Maker. When we are able to look into His eyes and answer His question, "Where are you?"

There is only One person that can tell you or me our reason for existing, our purpose and who we really are. This is something that we cannot discover for ourselves. It is not for us to discover. After all, we are the clay. There is only One person that knows what our real identity is supposed to be.

This is what we are trying to win; this is what will make our life journey rich and full of different textures and colors. The absolute glory of walking with God while he strips away the layers of sin to reveal the person you and I were meant to be is unsurpassed by any human endeavor that we can do. Everything else we do in life pales next to this. If we do not go on this journey, nothing else we do in life matters. This is the magnificent obsession, what was I *meant* to be, what was I *meant* to do, what was I *created* for? Only our Creator can answer that and He chooses to answer that question for us one person at a time.

So, if our whole point for being here is to find out why we are here and then do what we are supposed to do, why are there so many of us miserable with our lives? For those of us who have not discovered why we are here, I can understand the misery. But what about those of us who do know why we are here and we are still miserable? Life is just a struggle and we really do groan until the Lord comes, what is the problem here? Could it be that nothing is the problem? Could it be that we need to understand the Garden of Eden is closed?

Everything will not go our way, we will not be happy everyday, but if we stop and notice, we do have peace, we do have joy, the Lord has blessed us. Sometimes we just need to "buck up" and keep going. The campsite is not as comfortable as our bed at home. We are not at home, we are not supposed to be that comfortable, and sometimes we just need to quit whining. I really hate to put it that way, but my friends can testify, I do know how to whine. But I think that alone is why I can speak to my fellow whiners, IT WILL BE OKAY!! We just have to let go and let God, really!

The secret to the Christian life is to keep your eyes on Jesus. If you divert your eyes for one second, you see the storm and the big waves and you begin to sink. Until we see Him face-to-face, we will always be in a storm. So what is the strategy to win this race? It is to keep our eyes on Jesus. Everything will try to distract us from the one thing we are supposed to do which is to follow Jesus and grab whoever else wants to come along. Jesus was very serious when He said 'the road is strait (*hard*) and narrow and few there be that find it.' Any Christian that is one year or more in the Lord will tell you that it takes total concentration to follow the Lord. Fortunately for us, the Lord has left us "helps" so that we can be 'more than conquerors.'

One of the main "helps" is the Holy Spirit. I am not talking about speaking in tongues. I am not talking about getting delivered. I am talking about the person called the Holy Spirit otherwise known as the One who searches the *deep* things of God. The Holy Spirit will lead us into a deeper awareness of God if we allow Him. God is always doing something with us, to us or for us, but often we are not aware of it. Often we are not even aware of His presence. Prayer with the Holy Spirit guiding us will lead us into a constant awareness. The more aware we are of God, the more comfortable we will be around Him. The more comfortable we are around Him, the more likely we will begin to open up to Him and begin to share our life with Him.

Draw me after You and let us run together! SS 1:4

When we begin to share our life with Him, we begin to be irresistibly drawn closer because He really is "all that." The closer we draw to God, the more we see that He is holy; we begin to see that He is kind and full of grace. We begin to see and believe that He knows all about us and He loves us anyway. We begin to believe that we are accepted. We begin to see these things because He shares His life with us, also. We begin to have a relationship with Him.

The more aware we become of God in our life we begin to see the truth because, now, we begin to take on His attributes. Once we begin to see, we begin to worship Him. It is a natural response and it is nothing that is forced. As we dwell more in the Spirit and the Truth, the by-product is that we see who He really is and worship just begins. The 24 elders in heaven could not restrain themselves from falling down on their faces while they were in His presence because they saw Him in truth and we will do the same, also. The four beings that are around the throne have eyes all over their bodies (*constantly aware*) and all they do *night and day* is worship Him. When we go to prayer and we draw near to Him, that is what we will do, also.

As we begin to take on the mind of Christ, we will start to realize that our discernment becomes sharper. Since we dwell more in the Truth, any non-truth stands out. We begin to realize things that are not of His character. Most importantly of all, we begin to hesitate running after sin because we do not want to hurt or disappoint *our* Friend. Now the Christian life begins to take on a richness that was never before noticed. We are choosing not to sin because we know it will offend our Friend instead of it being "not lawful." We begin to walk in the Spirit and not the letter of the Law. Oh, praise be to God that He can call the dead back to life from darkness to light!!

As we spend more time with Him and we grow more confident in His acceptance of us, we find that we do not cower as much from the enemy as we used to. We do not doubt the Lord in the face of the storm as we used to. Surprisingly, we find ourselves standing when the enemy throws those darts at us. When we feel like we are being overwhelmed or when fear comes, it becomes more *natural* to run to *our* Friend. We discover that He really does know how to comfort us in our time of need. We discover that His Word *can* be very specific to our need. We discover that we *do* have a God worthy of our praise. Of course, the by-product of all this is that our faith grows and grows and grows. **This is what the enemy fears.**

We also discover that when we are in the Spirit we have authority. We begin to walk like we are the crowning glory of creation. We no longer walk like *mere* men.

We also become aware of how full of sin we really are. We are now living in the Light and the blemishes stand out. Beloved, it is okay, the Lord knows us, and He accepts us. We have to learn to accept ourselves. We are what we are - in this life. We are what we are – in Christ.

As we watch other saints in the Body it is easy to begin to covet or desire the gifts that they have. We often measure our weaknesses against our brother's strength. Each one of us has a vital part in the Lord's plan. In the flesh, without God we will always sin but, remember, we are a new creation. Beloved, we have been born again. We are new. We have been grafted in. As we spend more time in His presence, we begin to understand Him more and we begin to believe in that blood that was shed. We begin to believe in the power of that blood to cleanse us, totally. We also understand that our new life was given to us, that we did nothing to earn it. We learn humility. We learn how to say thank you.

Once we enter this realm of our walk, this will be when the attacks start getting vicious. It is at this point that you become dangerous to the enemy. You see, he realizes that now you are beginning to understand who you really are and, more importantly, who God is. This is the time that when you witness to someone about Christ, the person can clearly see that you are talking about a Person, not a religion. This is the time when you begin to believe that you really can sit in on the daily briefings. This is the time when you have ears to hear the daily briefings. What is the first rule of faith?

And without faith it is impossible to please Him, for he who comes to God must believe that He is, and that He is a rewarder of those who seek Him. Heb.11:6

Now we have to understand that winning may not look like winning. When Jesus died on the cross, that really did not look like He won anything and yet, He won everything. The Apostle Paul never really looked like he was winning when he was getting stoned, whipped and shipwrecked. When our life begins to go topsy-turvy, that is not the time to panic. When the saints were getting sawn in two, I am sure they did not count that a double blessing. In fact, the real strategy to winning never looks like you are winning except to the Lord.

I will say it again, if you do not have a relationship with the Lord you cannot swim in these waters. You will be overwhelmed and quickly swim back to shallower waters. Remember the sons of Sceva?

Jesus said, "Blessed are you when men cast insults at you, and persecute you, and say all kinds of evil against you falsely, on account of Me. Rejoice, and be glad, for so they persecuted the prophets who were before you." Why would He say that if it were not going to happen? It is a nice scripture to read, it is a very hard scripture to experience. The only way you can rejoice when that happens will be because you know that you are really winning.

Are we really ready to walk with Him? If one of us goes to prison for righteousness sake the fact is that you will be branded an ex-con when you get out. The fact is that you will have a hard time getting a job. If the Lord should call one of us to a foreign mission field the fact is that we will not be living in comfort in the United States. The fact is that we will not have a big income or the big house to go with it.

Fact is not always reality. The fact is that Jesus was crucified but the reality is that He secured eternal life for all of us. For most of us, we sometimes think it is better to see Him from afar.

I was going through a trial that just would not end. I mean, the thing just dragged on. I explained to the Lord that I had gotten the point and we could move on, but He was in one of those persistent moods and He really did not listen to me. Or, maybe, it was just that He did not agree with my assessment of the situation. Anyway, before this trial ended, I understood something very important about the Kingdom - among the many things I learned during that trial. I learned that the Lord really does very few things instantaneously for the benefit of my schedule.

When the Lord told Noah it was going to rain and he should build an ark, it took 120 years to rain. When the Lord anointed David to be king over Israel, it was years before that happened. When Jesus told the Pharisees that the temple would be torn down, it was years before that happened. Everything the Lord says He will do, He does no matter how much time or how many generations have gone by. It did rain, David became king and the temple was torn down. I needed to understand that I might not *see* the victory or the blessing in what I would consider a sufficient amount of time, but that it would surely happen. I needed to understand that that is just how the Kingdom works. It does not run on my time.

Abraham received a promise that he never saw in the flesh but he knew it would happen because he considered the Source of that promise. Noah gave blessings to his sons after the flood and generations later, in Isaiah 66, the Lord remembered that blessing for the descendents of Noah. Noah never saw that in his flesh, but he won. Seeing is not believing. What we see is temporary - what we do not see is eternal.

My point is this; you can trust the strategy that you get from the Lord. It will be very specific and, whether you see it or not, you will win the victory. Being humble and blessing our enemies may not seem very strategic, but it is. Praying for those who curse us may not seem strategic to a battle, but we have to trust that the Lord knows what He is doing. We read about Job and it is a very encouraging story, but clearly, Job did not know that he was in a very important spiritual battle. The one thing Job had going for him was that he trusted the Lord 'though He slay me.' It really is that simple.

Chapter Six

Shadows Have No Substance

*And the light shines in the darkness, and the darkness
did not comprehend it. Jn.1:5*

All of us, who are human, live under a shadow. Most of us,
live under several shadows and our lives are dark and bleak. For
some of us, the shadow that we exist under is "needing to be
accepted and loved." For some of us, the shadow that we exist
under is "needing to be secure." Sometimes that security will take
the form of intimidation or power gathering or even by being
battered as a spouse. For some of us, the shadow that we exist
under is "anger" that is hiding a multitude of pain. For most of us
in the United States, a common shadow that we exist under and
think is normal is "debt." The shadow of debt can be very dark and
very bleak.

We all have different shadows covering our lives that will
cause us to choose different paths or make certain choices. Often
those paths and choices lead us to even darker shadows instead of
the hoped for light at the end of the tunnel.

Often times, we find ourselves trapped in the shadows by our
own making and, oftentimes, the enemy has lured us into the
shadows where he is most comfortable. The shadows are dark and
hidden away. If we were to somehow find a way out from under

the shadows, I wonder what our lives would look like? If we could live knowing that we were accepted, knowing that we were loved and needed; that knowledge would produce very confident and sure humans. The confidence would not be something that we strive after or force; it would be as natural and comfortable as our own skin.

The interesting thing with shadows is that they do not exist unless an object is blocking the light to *cause* the shadow. Take for instance the shadow of death. In Psalm 23 the psalmist says, "yea, though I walk through the valley of the shadow of death..." and then he goes on to say, "I will fear no evil for You are with me." If death is blocking the Light that is causing a shadow, there is nothing to fear. The darker and sharper the shadow means that the Light is closer to the object. In fact, if we peek around death, the Light will hit us full in the face.

You might be saying to yourself, "well, that is fine, but death is *blocking* the Light." If you notice, the psalmist only talks about the "shadow of death." Why is that? Could it be that he knew death itself was nothing to fear for someone that walks with God? Beloved, shadows have no substance; there *is* nothing to fear.

A few years back, my mother passed away from cancer. We were never close but in her later years the Lord did work a substantial healing between us. When she was getting close to passing away, I was split between what was better; having her pass away quickly because dying from cancer is a painful way to die or having the Lord heal her. I could not pray with my full heart concerning the healing because her life was a painful one for her to live. She was reaping several seeds that she had sown in her earlier life and it was painful for me to watch. Anyway, as her time got closer, I was glad that the decision was the Lord's and not mine. The night before she passed, the Lord gave me a picture (*vision*) to share with her.

I had a picture of a baby coming down the birth canal and the father, doctor and nurses were waiting with much anticipation for the baby to come out. The baby did not have a clue what was happening. The only thing the baby knew was that it was comfortable one minute and the next minute it was being pushed and shoved down this canal. I was given the sense that Heaven is the same way. I shared this with my mother to comfort her with the comfort the Lord had given me.

The Lord, His angels and everyone else up there are waiting with much anticipation for us to arrive in the next life. We have no clue what is happening. All we know is that in this life we are quite comfortable and then death happens. We live most of our lives in death's shadow. Most of the things we do are because of death's shadow.

We spend our lives trying to be as comfortable or as powerful as we can be before we die. We all know that death will happen to each one of us someday. Some of us try to stay young as long as possible, as if death does not take the young also. Some of us try to feel alive with several lovers and/or husbands as we try to ignore that shadow. Some of us go overboard on the exercise and fitness routine, as if death does not take the strong and fit. We all have different ways to "tune out" the one thing that is on every human's mind; I will die someday.

For those of us that are actually allowed to reach those graying years, we seldom perceive what a grace the Lord has granted us. We start to slow down, things begin to ache and we begin to wrinkle, of all things! The Lord is kind enough to give us subtle warnings to get our house in order. Naturally, what we tend to do is go into deep, deep denial. All things in this life pass and we are not any different.

You who have been borne by Me from birth, and have been carried from the womb; even to your old age, I shall be the same, and even to your graying years I shall bear you! Is.46:3-4

Probably the most unnerving thing about death is that we have no control over it. Some of us try to take control by choosing our time of death, but the fact that we have to choose it at all shows that we have no control over it. No human knows what happens after death *for sure*. No one has come back to tell us about it.

Except One.

We have various religions that offer us a second chance to come back to *this* life. I don't know why anyone would want to take this ride again. Some religions offer "nirvana" or a continuous orgasmic experience if you are the right sex. I only know of one religion that takes "life after death" out of that hazy, nebulous fog and puts concrete specifics into the subject. That is probably because only one religion knows **exactly** what happens after death. Of course, I am talking about Christianity.

Jesus and His apostles were quite specific about what happens to humans after they die. Jesus specifically addresses that issue in every gospel. He knows what concerns humans the most even if we try to ignore the issue. He specifically says that He is the resurrection and the life. No human will resurrect without Him, plain and simple. I know most people think Jesus was a good man, even a prophet, but a good man would not say that, and a prophet would not dare think that.

Christianity tells humans very graphically what we can expect to see when we arrive. Christianity tells us very specifically what will happen when we take our last breath on earth and our first breath in Heaven. Christianity tells us what the major metropolis in the next age will look like specifically; with measurements, with colors and even what some of the structures will be made of. Christianity tells us what some of the animals will be in the next age. Christianity goes so far as to mention that we will even have a feast with the King of kings.

For those of us living under the shadow, Christianity is meant to give hope, a hope of glory. If Christianity were not true, it has to be one of the cruelest hoaxes released on mankind. For someone to come up with a story that is so detailed is beyond a lie; it must be the truth. Of course it doesn't have to be.

There are other choices for us that live under the shadow. We could believe that we were reincarnated. The only problem with that is that most people reincarnated were past kings or lords or queens and princesses, some type of noble born person. All those people that were the serfs, peasants and slaves, weren't they reincarnated also? My thought is that even kings and queens despair of life from time to time, so why go through it again? Life is hard with a few joyous bumps.

We could believe in the "good deeds outweigh the bad deeds" theory. Most religions have some version of that. We could be one of the most self-centered people on the planet, but as long as we give money to feed the unwashed masses, that should tip the scales in our favor. Right? If we give some money to open a few homeless shelters or even give our blood to help the sick that should really tip the scales in our favor. If we believe there is a god and if we believe that he is like that, how do we know that we will not die before we are able to tip the scales in our favor? What if we don't tip them enough?

Of course what I described is called "hedging the bet", and we humans do that with a finesse that is unbelievable. If we believe enough to hedge our bet, why don't we just ask God what He wants of us? Why do we have to complicate matters with our fears that come from our ignorance?

The other option is not to believe in anything but ourselves. No matter what comes our way we will handle it. When death comes, we will just die and that will be that. The only problem with that is, if we are wrong, of course, then that will be that.

> *And He made from one, every nation of mankind to live on all the face of the earth, having determined their appointed times, and the boundaries of their habitation, that they should seek God, if perhaps they might grope for Him and find Him, though He is not far from each one of us; for in Him we live and move and exist. Acts 17: 26-28*

This was our situation; we were hopelessly lost, doomed to dwell in the shadow of death, then die and have an excruciatingly painful eternity. God had already pronounced judgment, the spear had already left His hand and it was flying through the air, aimed at us.

Then Jesus stepped in front of us. He took the spear for us. He died.

And then, and then, and then He came back to life; death could not hold Him. And now, death cannot touch Him.

WOW!!!

Jesus took our main fear and crushed it!

That is the truth of it people. We did not have enough good deeds to outweigh our bad deeds. No amount of ignoring death was going to make it go away. We could choose to worship whatever we wanted to worship. But the fact remains, only one person stepped in between God's judgment and us, and that was Jesus.

Ever since then, the shadow has not had any substance! Death has been defeated. We can continue to fear, we can continue to run and hide, but it is not necessary. In fact, it is a bit foolish since we don't have to. Of course, we can believe whatever we want to believe. I could give you a check for one thousand dollars but it will not do you any good unless you believed it was good and you cashed it. Beloved, Jesus has given us the check. We just have to believe it is good and cash it.

Living out from under the shadow is a marvelous way to live. You feel the Son's light on you and it is warm. It is good and wholesome. You see the vivid colors of life, you breathe in deep gulps of life. Life's troubles come, heartaches come, pain is still a part of life, but it is different when you are in the Light. You *know* everything will be okay. Deep in your spirit you have a peace and a joy that even you do not understand. When your world falls apart, you are still able to stand because you live in the Light and that makes all the difference in this world and in the one to come.

Jesus says, "I have come that you might have life and life more abundantly."

Beloved, once we grasp what has been accomplished for us, the enemy will flee whenever he can. Why was the apostle Paul so focused on serving Jesus? Paul understood that because of Jesus, he did not have to be Saul. Paul was a murderer of the saints! The Bible does not speak to this but, since humans will be humans, don't you think that some cities Paul went into, he ran into people that hated him because he had their father or mother or son killed? Don't you think there were some Jews that couldn't stand to see the Holy Spirit using Paul so powerfully? Paul had to deal with those issues. Paul *had* to believe he was a new creation because there was nothing he could do to tip the scales in his favor; he had nowhere else to go. This had to be a man that *knew* he was forgiven much. He understood that he had been saved; he understood that he was free; he understood that he was loved. The same is there for us; we were all made in His image and He died for each one of us.

We spend our lives pacing our cages not even noticing that the door is open. The enemy knows it is open and he tries to keep us distracted so we won't notice the open door. What do you think he would do if we walked out of the cage? Jesus has given us the authority to command the devil to exit out of our lives. Jesus has given us the power to say "no" to sin. We just have to cash it in. We are rich, beloved, but we live like paupers. That is foolish. We are strong and mighty in His power, yet we cower in the corner. We need to walk out from under the shadow into His marvelous light. Let's find the sunglasses.

Chapter Seven

How Not to be Blindsided

Search me, O God, and know my heart; try me and know my anxious thoughts. Ps. 139:23

Well, what if you are doing all the right things and you still get blindsided by the enemy? If you were doing all of the right things, you would not get blindsided by the enemy. If you believe that you are doing all you can and you are still getting blindsided, you are calling God a liar. I know that sounds harsh but that is really what you are doing. God says that He has given us everything we need to walk victoriously, to be more than conquerors, in Him. Unfortunately, it is not a common sight to see a victorious Christian. As I have mentioned earlier, most Christians believe the enemy. We may not say that with our lips but our lives often shout the fact. If we believe the enemy and not God, who has the whole truth, how can we expect not to be blindsided? The enemy will never do us right. Let me give you a typical example of how we are so often blindsided.

You wake up early Sunday morning to spend time with the Lord before you get ready to go to church. You and the Lord have a wonderful time. Worship is rich and full. During your prayer time you feel like the Lord is giving you an anointing to pray. Your time in the Word is revelation after revelation. Oh, it was a glorious time and you thank the Lord accordingly. As you reluctantly leave the throne room to get ready for church, you are enjoying a wonderful afterglow.

You begin to hum to yourself 'Our God Reigns' and, of course, halfway through the shower you are belting it out to the Lord. Oh yes, it is a glorious day! You proceed to get dressed and you are still humming 'Our God Reigns' as you get into your car to make your way to your Father's house. You pull out of the driveway and you crank up your stereo that has some suitable worship music on and you proceed to drive to church so you can join in with the rest of the Body in worship to your magnificent God! Halfway there, you notice some red and blue lights in your rearview mirror. As you pullover, the car with the red and blue lights pulls over also. Hmmm.

It is Friday afternoon; you went to work early so you could get off early because of the Bible study retreat for the weekend. You have been looking forward to this for two months. You know you are in for some good teaching and you will have a chance to spend a lot of time with the Lord. You are looking forward to what He will share with you, not to mention time for some really good fellowship. You stop by your house to pick up your luggage that has been packed for two days, now. You get in your car so you can drive over to where you will meet everyone else who is going.

On the drive over, you remember something you forgot to tell your friend who would be feeding your cat while you are gone so you pull over to a phone booth. You call your friend and give her *more* information on how to take care of your cat for the next two days and, because she is a new creation also, she politely listens. You finish the conversation and hop back into your car and take off. Six blocks later you remember that you left your wallet on the ledge beneath the phone in the phone booth. You do a U-turn in traffic and speed back to the phone booth; the wallet is not there. Hmmm.

As some of you know, those situations are more common than we care to admit. How many of us will have a glorious time in church and, on the way home, be fighting with our spouse before we are even out of the church parking lot? It is a common occurrence and it need not be if we just remember one thing. We are drunk.

I would like to be able to have something more complex to say, something deep, but, oh well. There is nothing wrong with being drunk in the Spirit. It is a glorious thing but we have to remember that we have an enemy that is just waiting for us to let our guard down. The apostle Peter tells us to be of sober spirit, walk circumspectly. When we get drunk in the Spirit we need to stay in a safe place for a while until we "come down" a little bit and then proceed on with whatever we are about. If we have a glorious time in prayer, which I pray we all do, maybe we should just sit in the Lord's presence for a while. We all know that in His presence is fullness of joy so we do not have to rush out. It is possible that as we sit there quietly the Lord might share something more with us. Or maybe He just wants to sit with you enjoying *your* presence. What a concept.

My point is that we always have to remember that we are in enemy territory and the enemy will take any opportunity to steal our joy or distract us from our pursuit of the Kingdom. When we are drunk in the Holy Spirit, our emotions are running rampant and we are not very alert. Again, I am not saying to refrain from having a good time in the Spirit. I am saying hang out with the Spirit a little bit longer until we are able to have sober judgment again. He is fully aware of all the things you have to do for that day, He is fully aware of when you have to be at work or when you have to drop the kids off for day care. He is also fully aware of how the enemy hates you and wants to harm you.

Remember; while we are on this planet we just have to occupy ourselves. Our main goal is not to be the best employee or the hardest working employee. Our main goal is not to be the best spouse and the most diligent parent. Our main goal on this planet is to please the Lord. The other things will be by-products of that. You will be a good employee, you will be a good spouse and parent but only *because* you are following hard after the Lord. As we run around doing all these things that occupy our time, we have to remember that the time we do set aside for the Lord can be an overwhelming experience for our emotions. He is God after all.

Thou are the God, Thou alone, of all the kingdoms of the earth. Thou hast made heaven and earth. 2Kings 19: 15b

Sometimes you can sit and have a cup of tea with Him and just enjoy a mellow time. Other times you wonder if He is even in the house. And then there are those times when He draws near and all you can do is fall flat on your face because He overwhelms you. It is those times that you need to just sit with Him awhile. God has just short-circuited your emotional make-up and you have to realize that it will take a little time to come back online. And that is okay. It really is. To have a foretaste of Heaven is really okay.

While all that is going on, the enemy and his cronies are fully aware that you are basking in His presence. What do you think they will do as soon as you give them an opportunity? Beloved, Jesus gave us the armor for a reason.

There are other ways you can be blindsided if you are not alert and wise to the enemy's schemes.

You and your spouse were really touched by the pastor's teaching on spending more quality time with your children. Both of you talk about it and come up with a wonderful idea. Instead of Daddy and Mommy watching television after dinner and the kids playing video games, you two think it would be great to read a story each night. Not just any story but something that would build Christian character into your kids. Daddy will read a chapter or two each night. You both take it to prayer and it seems the Lord is pleased with the idea. You share it with the kids and since they really can't veto the idea, it is a go. You will start tomorrow night.

The next morning the alarm doesn't go off and hubby is late for work. While you are cooking breakfast for the kids, the toast gets stuck in the toaster. They end up having Pop Tarts and they run off late for school. As you are cleaning up the kitchen and washing the dishes, your wedding ring slips off your finger and down into the garbage disposal. You call hubby on his cell phone and with much anxiety tell him what happened and he says, without much feeling, to call the plumber. In a huff you hang up on the insensitive brute. Meanwhile...

You (hubby) finally make it to work and as you are taking the elevator up to your office, you realize that the report that you were going to finalize today for the presentation tomorrow is not in your briefcase. You get off the elevator and walk down the hall and your assistant says good morning and asks you if you remembered the early morning breakfast meeting with the staff. You stop dead in your tracks and just stare. It completely slipped your mind.

Both of you manage to get through your respective days until hubby comes home. The plumbing bill was quite a bit higher than expected and you are really irritated at her for "dropping" the ring down the disposal anyway. She is quite irritated with you because you obviously don't care about the marriage since you could care less if she lost the ring or not. The kids are just staying in the basement playing video games. Hmmm.

Let's get a little closer to home. You faithfully go to church every Sunday unless, of course, you are on vacation or sick. You faithfully read and pray. You have two wonderful kids that are 11 and 14 years of age. You have a wonderful husband who works hard and provides well for the family - at least that is what is presented outside of the home. Inside the home is anything but peace, love and joy.

Your finances have always been tight because you insisted to your husband that the kids had to go to Christian schools. The bathroom needed to be redone and somehow it took all of the money that you both have been saving for the down payment on a new home. Hubby *needed* that new extended cab pickup "for the family." Your first family vacation had to be to Disney World instead of some local campsite. The kids always heard the arguments about the finances and they just learned to stay in their room playing videos.

Daddy never could get very affectionate with the kids. His upbringing was not much different. It never occurred to him to tell his girls how pretty they were or how much he loved them. The girls knew that Jesus loved them but they were never too sure about Daddy. He never noticed the fourteen year old as she was growing up doing things to irritate him just to get his attention. He was too focused on the finances. Mom saw it and would often talk to him about it but the conversation fell on dull ears because Mom always told him, or implied, that everything he did was wrong anyway.

Of course, time stops for no one. The kids continue to grow and now they are 14 and 17 years old. Now they are feeling their own power. They are aware that they can seek refuge outside of the home. And they do. They want nothing to do with Christianity or Jesus because they saw that it did not make a difference in their own family. Mom and Dad have that nice big new home. Dad has another new pickup and Mom still faithfully goes to church every Sunday. Hmmm.

Oh come on; let's bring it home. You faithfully go to church every Sunday. Your husband is in the military but wherever he is stationed, you both find a Bible believing church to go to. Hubby is esteemed in the church and even leads the men's bible study. You are the sweet, submissive wife. Your four kids are raised up in the church. They do extremely well in school. You and hubby don't really have a very affectionate marriage but it's to late to back out now. It never occurs to either of you to tell your kids that you love them - they should just know that.

The house is run in military fashion, all the kids have their chores, and discipline is the order of the day. Your kids are spaced two years apart; three girls and the oldest, a boy. The youngest is ten. The youngest comes into puberty and hubby begins to molest her as he did the other daughter that you stayed in denial about. There is no denial with this one because she screams every time he comes into her bedroom. Everyone keeps faithfully going to church.

Hubby and family move to different places according to where he is stationed by the military. Time rolls on.

The ten year old is now twelve and she is feeling her power. She knows that what Daddy is doing is wrong. She knows that her family will not help her; home is not a refuge but something to run from. She runs. She runs from Christianity and Jesus, also.

Dad continues on in the military and the church. You are still the sweet, submissive wife. The oldest daughter is strung out on cocaine. The second oldest daughter has a child out of wedlock and is an alcoholic. The boy is married now and his wife wears the pants in the family. Oh, and the youngest, no one has heard from. Hmmm.

These are the dirty little secrets that are never shared in the Body. These are the things that only the Lord knows about. When Johnny shows up in Sunday school with a swollen eye and a cut lip, we accept the lie that he has been instructed to tell us. When Susie suddenly has a drastic change of personality, she is now sullen and quiet whereas she used to be perky and quick to laugh, we do not inquire too deeply. Joey always shows up in the same unwashed clothes every Sunday and he is always reluctant to leave when class is over. Beloved, the enemy is having a heyday while we are being polite. If we confront sin in the early stages, it does not have a chance to grow into the monster that it will surely be.

Then when lust has conceived, it gives birth to sin; and when sin is accomplished, it brings forth death. Jam.1:15

Each one of the previous situations are all too common. We all can think of many tragedies that we have heard of or have been a part of. Each situation started with a brother or sister not being alert. The Lord warned Cain in Genesis "sin is crouching at the door, and its desire is for you, but you must master it." Sin is always crouching at our door. We must never forget that. Peter and Paul warn us to be sober and alert for these things:

➤   Alert for prayer – I Pet. 4:7

➤   Alert for warfare – I Pet. 5:8

➤   Alert for ministry – 2 Tim. 4:5

➤   Alert so darkness will not overtake us – I Thes. 5:6

We need to be alert or we will be blindsided by the enemy and our flesh will only complicate matters. So many things we allow into our lives that wreak havoc in the end. Why do you think the Lord shortened the days for the elect? This is not a time to slack off or be casual about following after the Lord. This is as serious as it gets and Jesus is very serious about His bride. The real question is, how serious are we about our Bridegroom?

Let the righteous smite me in kindness and reprove me, it is oil upon the head; do not let my head refuse it. Ps. 141:5

Somehow we must get to a place where we put our pride aside and share with our brothers and sisters about the things we struggle with and *especially* the ugly things we struggle with. We were not meant to walk alone. We are a Body. We also must get to a place where we are willing to be uncomfortable with our brother or sister while we confront them about their sin or their actions that will lead to sin. The enemy counts on us being too uncomfortable to say anything while he leads someone to hell.

This does not mean that we go ripping people apart. It means that we LOVE them enough to pull them back from the fire. That is what love is. It is fine to hug and have the potlucks and share scripture but will we lay our life down for our brother or sister? Will we get uncomfortable for their sakes? Before we confront someone, we need to bathe the conversation in prayer because what we say or don't say could knock him or her off the path. Ephesians 6:18 says that with all perseverance and petition to pray for all the saints. We must pray for our other brothers and sisters. It is vital. It is not a time for haughtiness, piousness or patronization. It is a time for rescue. Just as Jesus so often rescues us.

This is the walk, this is the fight, this is the glory of being in the Body, "and they will know us by the love we have one for another."

Chapter Eight

Blocking With the Shield

A man can receive nothing unless it has been given him from heaven. Jn. 3:27

For most soldiers that are in battle, they have some type of shield to block the blows of their opponent - sort of like extra protection. When Paul is talking about putting on the armor of God, he is using the Roman soldier as an example for us. The Roman shield was a large oblong or oval piece, approximately four feet high by two feet wide, made of wood and leather, often with an iron frame. Sometimes the leather would be soaked in water to help extinguish *fiery arrows*. The ancient "flaming arrow" or "fire dart" was made of cane with a flammable head that was lighted and then shot so as to set fire to wooden shields, cloth tents, etc.

For Christians, this shield is faith—absolute and complete reliance on God. Faith means total dependence on God and our *willingness* to do His will. It is not something we put on for a show for others. It means believing in His promises even though we don't see those promises materializing *yet*. When the enemy sends his fiery arrows of temptation, doubt, wrath, lust, despair, vengeance, problems, and trials into our lives, we can hold up our shields and stop them. Faith gives us the strength to stand against Satan with a firm, unyielding courage, even when he uses his most fearsome weapons.

The Lord has not left us defenseless. We seldom use our shield properly but we do have a shield that we are supposed to be using. Some of us think our faith is a heavenly debit card. With enough faith, we can draw on our riches in heaven for our earthly comforts. Some of us think our faith is a shield to protect us from the trials of living in a fallen world such as sickness, unemployment, despair and so forth. We all admit that, indeed, the Lord did give us each a measure of faith; we just get a little confused on what we are supposed to do with it.

Well, since it is a gift from Jesus to us, the first thing to do is to accept it and say thank you. Faith is one of those gifts where the more we use it the more it grows. Somewhat like a muscle. Hmm. Now, where have we heard that? In spiritual warfare, faith is extremely important because it enables us to block the blows of the enemy and even push him back a few feet. I think it is hard to block a blow that you do not see coming, though. I will attempt to give some examples of what some of the blows from the enemy look like in everyday life so we all can recognize them in our own lives. I am all for shining light in the dark places.

You have just graduated from high school and you are looking forward to going to college. You are not sure what your major will be but you think being a lawyer sounds good plus it pays well. With much excitement, you sign up for a Business Law class along with your other classes. The term begins; college is new and exciting; you are getting to know several people. One night while you are at home doing your homework, a family member walks by and sees you doing your homework. You happen to be doing the

Business Law homework. The only thing they can think to say is, "anyone can be a lawyer." POW!

You are in your mid-fifties and you have only been saved for a couple of years. The Lord is so sweet and you have the same kind of zeal, wonder and awe that most young Christians have just getting saved. You are definitely in the midst of that "born again high." The Bible is exciting, you can't get enough teaching and life is just great! Praise the Lord! You feel like you have a definite call to go to seminary. You are not sure the Lord is calling you to be a pastor but you know that you should go to seminary to learn more of the Word.

Since you are new to the faith, you think it would be wise to talk this over with someone who has walked with the Lord a lot longer than you have. After church on the next Sunday, you ask this brother that is esteemed in the church if he would like to join you for a cup of coffee. He says okay. After both of you have settled into the booth in the coffee shop, you share with him what is on your heart about going to seminary. He thinks that is a great idea but then he asks you, "don't you think you are a little too old to be going to seminary?" Oomph!

You go to a Bible study once a week with some wonderful sisters. One of the sisters, who is considered one of the pillars in your church, has taken you under her wing. You are growing and you feel grateful to God that He had someone come along side you in your walk. A couple of years pass and you and the sister are quite close but it is not really a friendship on an even playing field. You are the one that is being ministered to all the time and you would like to help carry her burdens also and for her to share her life with you. At your next meeting, you share these feelings with the sister and she responds, "we are not on the same level, that can't happen." Ouch! That knocked you on the ground!

These are all examples of sincere Christians trying to find their way on planet earth in the Kingdom of Heaven. As you can see, the enemy takes full advantage of their naiveté.

Let's go to something more controversial like Creation versus Evolution. You are in college - it is your second year and one of the required classes that you have to take is Philosophy. The professor that teaches the class is known for putting students through the ringer that confess that they are Christians. You have tried to sign with other professors that are teaching Philosophy, but the classes have either been full or they did not fit your schedule. With much trembling, you show up for class on the first day of the term. The first thing out of the Professor's mouth after he takes attendance is, "who in this room is a Christian?" It is totally silent and four hands slowly rise into the air; one of the hands is yours. The Professor tells four other students who are sitting in the front row to switch seats with "the Christians."

For the next six weeks, the four of you are hammered, humiliated, laughed at and generally made fools of for your convictions. The Professor's favorite topic is how ludicrous the "creation belief" is and only people without much intelligence believe in it. The Professor patiently explains to the four of you how absurd it is to believe that the universe was created in six 24-hour days. You faithfully point out to him that the Bible says "and there was evening and there was morning", which clearly shows a 24-hour day. The Professor does not even bother answering the statement.

Each evening the four of you get together and have a grumbling session about the Professor. After one of the grumbling sessions, one of your fellow Christians comes up to you and says that maybe one day of creation *is* really a thousand years and maybe it took God six thousand years to make the universe. POW!

Let's go back to the Christian that was on the fast track in the corporation until they witnessed to one their managers. You have stood strong through the trial; you have drawn closer to the Lord and the result is a more focused lifestyle. You have returned to the Body and you are a committed member. The co-workers on your job are talking to you now but you have been reassigned to "special projects."

So far, the only thing you have been assigned is typing old outdated company policies – that's it – day in and day out. You have been taken off most of the email lists and you are not asked to attend any of the department or company meetings. You are the last one to hear about what the department is doing. Everyone in your department, including the people that you used to supervise, all know that the only thing that you do now is type outdated company policies. The joke *that you have learned* to laugh at is that you are the department secretary. Oomph!

All of these situations are situations that the enemy takes full advantage of. The enemy knows how skilled you are with your shield.

But the Lord...

He did this to teach warfare to generations of Israelites who had no experience in battle. Judg. 3:2 NLT

We all take hits but some of those hits are because of our lack of skill at using our shield. I tell brothers and sisters all the time that are new to the faith to "get to know that Bible." You need to *know* the Word; the living and the written Word. The Word is the foundation of our walk; it needs to be solid and strong so we can overcome the world, the evil one and ourselves. We need to be saturated in the Word; for the saints in the U.S. we have no excuse not to be.

So, what is this shield of faith? Well, think of it like a force field around your spirit and your mind. We live what we believe. For example, the day before Halloween, on Oct. 30, 1938, when millions of Americans tuned in to a popular radio program that featured plays directed by, and often starring, Orson Welles, the performance that evening was an adaptation of the science fiction novel *The War of the Worlds*, about a Martian invasion of the earth. But in adapting the book for a radio play, Welles made an important and history making change: under his direction, the play was written and performed so it would sound like a news broadcast about an invasion from Mars, a technique that, presumably, was intended to heighten the dramatic effect.

As the play unfolded, dance music was interrupted a number of times by fake news bulletins reporting that a "huge flaming object" had dropped on a farm near Grovers Mill, New Jersey. As members of the audience sat on the edge of their seats, actors played news announcers, officials and other roles one would expect to hear in a news report. They described the landing of an invasion force from Mars and the destruction of the United States. The broadcast also contained a number of disclaimers that it was all a radio play, *but* if members of the audience missed a brief explanation at the beginning, the next one didn't arrive until 40 minutes into the program.

At one point in the broadcast, an actor in a studio, playing a newscaster in the field, described the emergence of one of the aliens from its spacecraft. "Good heavens, something's wriggling out of the shadow like a gray snake," he said, in an appropriately dramatic tone of voice. "Now it's another one, and another. They look like tentacles to me. There, I can see the thing's body. It's large as a bear and it glistens like wet leather. But that face. It...it's indescribable. I can hardly force myself to keep looking at it. The eyes are black and gleam like a serpent. The mouth is V-shaped with saliva dripping from its rimless lips that seem to quiver and pulsate. The thing is rising up. The crowd falls back. They've seen enough. This is the most extraordinary experience. I can't find words. I'm pulling this microphone with me as I talk. I'll have to stop the description until I've taken a new position. Hold on, will you please, I'll be back in a minute."

As the audience listened to this simulation of news broadcast, created with voice acting and sound effects, a portion of the audience concluded that it was hearing an actual news account of an invasion from Mars. People packed the roads, hid in cellars, loaded guns, even wrapped their heads in wet towels as protection from Martian poison gas, in an attempt to defend themselves against aliens, oblivious to the fact that they were acting out the role of the panic-stricken public that actually belonged in a radio play. * People were stuck in a kind of virtual world in which *fiction was confused for fact.*

News of the panic (which was conveyed via genuine news reports) quickly generated a national scandal. This is a clear example of "you live what you believe." Now can you imagine what would happen if we began to believe in the Word of God? I think amazing things would begin to happen. We would see things as they truly are. In the examples above, instead of doubling over when we would get hit, the hits would just bounce off us; they would be unable to penetrate because we know the truth!

When a family member says to you that anyone can be a lawyer, instead of that comment penetrating, you would *believe* the Word when it says that He has created good works for *you* to walk in and you are just being faithful. When a sincere brother tells you that you are too old to go to seminary, you *believe* the Word that says that He will restore the years that the locusts have eaten. Beloved, we must stand on the Word and trust God that He will be faithful to His Word. As you watch Him stay faithful to His Word, *your* confidence and trust (*faith*) grows in the Evidence that is displayed in your life. You don't need to see to believe – YOU KNOW.

When your professor hammers at you in class and you are not *yet* skilled or knowledgeable enough to give a reasonable answer, you still KNOW that God would never lie. You were not there at the beginning of creation but you KNOW if God said it, it must be true. You do not have to fret that the Bible may be found out to be a fraud. Abraham was told he was going to have a son; he was very old; but Abraham figured if God said it that is all that mattered. Abraham would not be able to explain *how* he would be able to bear a son at that age but he did not need to explain, he just needed to believe God.

> *...let God be found true, though every man be found a liar... Rom.3:4*

Many times the enemy will throw stuff at us that we really cannot explain; the how and the why and that is okay, we just need to believe God. The details will get worked out later. Things that rocked my faith in my early years of Christianity don't even faze me now because my faith has grown and I have become more skilled with my shield. God has promised us that our shield is able to extinguish *all* of the fiery darts that the enemy throws at us. We need to believe God and trust in the weapons that He gives us. Practice makes good, a lot of practice makes very good. God has promised to establish us and He will be faithful to do just that.

> *But solid food is for the mature, who because of practice have their senses trained to discern good and evil. Heb. 5:14*

You have to understand that trials will come. Everything will be going along fine, you are being obedient and then suddenly a crisis happens. They are never convenient and they seem to always take us by surprise. We are cautioned 'not to be amazed' when these trials happen. Of course, the first thing we are is amazed.

What saints often fail to realize is that the natural often is a shadow of the spiritual. For example, humans have certain stages of growth: baby, toddler, child, pre-teen, teen, young adult, adult, elderly. All humans have those exact same stages, of course several of us do not go through all of those stages mentally, but physically, that is how humans live. The same is true in the spiritual; there is a time when you are a baby, toddler, child, pre-teen, teen, young adult, adult and mature saint.

Many saints don't realize that you really do have to take time to grow and you really can't rush it. You just grow when you grow. The Lord gives the increase. You never really see a flower crying out to Heaven, "Lord, make me grow." No, of course not, it just grows. Some saints are flowers, some saints are bushes, and some saints are trees. If you are a tree, it may look like nothing is happening for years, but if you could see beneath the ground, you would see the roots steadily going deeper and deeper. The Lord made you what you are and you will grow accordingly. Trust Him. He has done this before, after all.

It is usually in our spiritual teen years that the Lord will start teaching us how to be skillful with our shield. Up to that time, we are usually eating, resting, playing and enjoying our time with the Lord, steadily growing, constantly feeding on the milk of the Word. During those early years, the Lord's presence is often *felt*, prayers are answered quickly, it is a very black and white world, it is just a great time in the Lord. If everything is going in a normal manner, the Lord begins to wean us off the *things that can be seen* and He begins to exercise our faith so we can grow strong... and then the teen years hit.

All I can say is that these are usually the dramatic years. Up until then it has been real cozy, a blessed time. The Lord has faithfully fed us and now He wants us to take on *some* responsibility and feed ourselves. We usually are getting pretty cocky by this time.

> *And the sons of Israel ate the manna forty years, until they came to an inhabited land, they ate the manna until they came to the border of the land of Canaan. Ex. 16:35*

Just like in the natural, this is the age we are starting to feel our power. We believe we know enough to make our own decisions with the Lord *assisting* us. The trials come, we get rebellious, we learn the deeper truths of repentance. Everything is a crisis. There is a lot of drama; our faith is up and down. Looking back, it is pretty humorous; going through it is another story. We also begin to think that we look pretty good, now that the Lord has straightened us out. He has renewed our mind so we can actually think straight and true.

This is a critical point in our walk, this is the time that we decide to go deeper or just try to stay on the sidelines. This is the time when we think we can do so many things in our own strength. These are the rough teen years when we find out what the walk will cost us and if we are willing to pay. These are the years that we become real busy with a lot of Christian activity. These are the years that we forget that our best buddy just a few years ago was Jesus and all we wanted to do then was hang out with Him. These are the years that we have a tendency to get so caught up in doing the Lord's work that we don't have time for Him. And of course, these are the years that the Lord has to break us so the oil of His Spirit can pour forth.

> *And the manna ceased on the day after they had eaten some of the produce of the land, so that the sons of Israel no longer had manna, but they ate some of the yield of the land of Canaan during that year. Jos. 5:12*

And these are also the years that we learn to fight. We learn what warfare is all about. We meet the Captain of the Hosts. These are the years that we learn what victory means, these are the years that we learn to flex our muscles.

And of course, these are the years that we learn that the battle is not ours to fight. We learn the painful lessons of running ahead of the Lord and the consequences of doing that. These are all needful lessons that *must* be learned, it is not the end of the world. Every saint goes through it. These are hard lessons to learn.

The "teen years" will be when our faith starts to be tested. Up until then the Lord fed us when we were hungry, gave us water when we were thirsty and gave us clothing and shelter. During the forty years that the Israelites were in the wilderness, they could on any given night step out of their tent and look towards the center of camp and see the Cloud of Fire. That must have been an awesome sight. They could *see* that the Lord was with them. The Lord had to mature that faith, they had to know that He was present always whether they saw the Cloud or not.

It is the same for us. Every trial or crisis that we go through is for one objective only – the testing of our faith. When trials happen in our marriage, our jobs or businesses, or our other relationships, the only purpose is for our faith to be revealed; whether it is lacking or not. Will we remain true to the Lord and His commands or not? Will we trust the Lord to work out the situation or not? Are we going to believe that the Cloud of Fire is still there to lead us through?

It is not by chance that the first conflict that the Israelites have in the Promised Land is Jericho. After they spy out the land and determine that they can conquer it, the Lord tells them what to do. He says to march around the city once a day, to not say a word, and to put the priests in the front of the line. Um, okay. I don't know any military strategist that would try this. I am sure, after the first couple of days, the Israelites were wondering when the Lord was going to do something. It must have been humiliating and they could not even complain! It is the same with us. The Lord tells us how to walk through our trial and it often *appears* foolish. Of course we start to wonder when the Lord is going to take care of the problem also. Now where did that Cloud go?

During most of my trials, the first thing I want to do is to go tell somebody how I am suffering. Often, the Lord just wants me to be quiet and not make a sound. Often, that is the last thing I do. A brother told me years ago a wise word and I have never forgotten it, "An absolute crisis absolutely reveals absolutely." If I ever want to see what I am made of, a trial will reveal what I really believe. Do I run to a friend when a crisis happens or do I run to the Lord? Hmmm.

Sometimes it is good to see what we are made of; sometimes we need to see what the measure of our faith is. Sometimes we find it is "wanting" and we need to press in to know the Lord more and have Him adjust a few things.

After the Israelites have marched around this city for six days, on the seventh day the Lord tells them to march around the city seven times, blow their horns and then give a shout. Many scholars over the years have said many things as to why the walls came tumbling down. My own opinion is that the Lord just knocked them down. I have been in many a trial and on those rare occasions where I actually listened to the Lord and obeyed Him, the following results defy any other explanation except that the Lord fought the battle for me. That's it. I could fool myself and say that it would have worked out eventually but then I would be living in deception and robbing the praise that is *due* the Lord.

I will say one last thing, well, maybe two things about Jericho. The Lord had the Israelites give the shout of victory before the walls fell down. They had to stretch their faith and trust that the Lord would do what He promised to do. The Lord asked them to praise Him for the victory before they saw the victory. When Jericho was conquered, the rewards were plentiful. The same goes for us when we trust and obey the Lord. The rewards are plentiful.

In 2 Chronicles chapter 20 you see a repeat of Jericho only it is King Jehoshaphat instead of Joshua. The Captain tells the Israelites the same thing, *"The battle is not yours, I will fight for you, station yourselves, stand and see the salvation of the Lord on your behalf."* King Jehoshaphat listens and obeys. The Israelites just stand there and the enemy is defeated. All they did was follow up afterward and pick up the spoils of the battle. We serve a good God.

It is interesting that in this battle, the worship leaders went before the army also. When they began singing and praising the Lord, that is when the Lord began setting the ambushes for the enemy. There is power in praise and the Lord delights to see our faith at work. If you are being overwhelmed in a trial, station yourself, begin praising the Lord and watch Him work.

When the Israelites entered the Promised Land, the Lord was asking them to grow up. Up until then they had been concerned with the Lord taking care of *their* needs. In the Promised Land, the Lord was asking them to *join Him* in His agenda; which was to conquer the land and glorify His name. Again, it is not any different with us. There comes a time when we must trust the Lord to take care of our needs while we go out to conquer the land and glorify His name. At some point in our walk, we must understand that it is His show and He has graciously asked us to partake in it.

We eventually learn that we really have nothing to contribute to the Lord but a broken and contrite spirit. We bounce from being cocky to being the lowest worm on the planet. But during this whole time, in our teen years, we are steadily growing, steadily taking in data, we are going from faith to faith, strength to strength and from one glory to another glory. Our skill with our shield grows day by day.

> *So let us know, let us press on to know the Lord. His going forth is as certain as the dawn; and He will come to us like the rain, like the spring rain watering the earth. Hos. 6:3*

Of course we don't see this, in fact, we don't really see any of this except in hindsight. But when we look back, we clearly see that the Lord was, is and will be faithful to establish us; to make us *more than* conquerors.

Chapter Nine

Thrusting With the Sword

And he took the mantle of Elijah that fell from him, and struck the waters and said, "Where is the Lord, the God of Elijah?" 2Kin. 2:14

Okay, we have the armor, we have the shield, now we need a weapon. A soldier without a weapon in the midst of a battle will not last very long. I'm sure we all know that. We all also know that our weapon is the sword of the Spirit, which is the Word of God. In the book of John when the guards came to take Jesus to the High Priest, Jesus said three words and the guards fell to the ground. That is the power of the Word. Of course we know that the Word alone holds together all of creation. We know planets follow their orbits in obedience to that Word. The ocean surf crashes against the sand of the beach and comes no further in obedience to the Word. We all know that lightning and thunder wait on the Word before they do anything.

Will you really annul My judgment? Will you condemn Me that you may be justified? Or do you have an arm

like God, and can you thunder with a voice like His?
Job 40:8-9

So often we do not pick up our sword, so often we allow our sword to get rusty and dull. So often we despise our weapon and then we wonder why we get beat up so often.

The way basketball player's handle a basketball is a phenomenal thing to watch. I am really not a fan but I do appreciate watching people use their skills at a high level. Anyway, if you watch the players, they handle that ball like it was a part of their hand. Often, they just think about what they want the ball to do and their hand is already translating the thought so that the ball will do just what they want. It really is an incredible thing to watch. I know that these players did not just walk out there one day and begin to handle the ball like that. It took years of practice.

I watch little kids bouncing a basketball down the street as they are on their way to wherever they are going and they look very clumsy with the ball. The ball is too big for their hands and they often have to use two hands to bounce the ball. As the years go on, they become familiar with the basketball. The ball becomes comfortable and natural in their hands. When they play basketball, just by virtue of habit, they train their thought and body to act as one so that the ball will do what they want it to do. Now of course they do not look at it like that. They are having fun. A few hone their skill to such a high level that they are able to make a living at it, but most players of the game are at least able to work up a sweat on a Saturday afternoon playing the game.

I am sure we all get the point, but just in case there is someone who does not, I will point out the point. We need to spend time in the Word and become comfortable and familiar with it. The Word is able to do anything but if you are unfamiliar with it, you leave the Spirit very little to work with. The Lord will do many things just to keep the honor of His name but He will do far more things if you are able to quote His Word to Him. It worked for Abraham and Moses and it will work for us.

The Lord loves to bless those who take delight in His Word. There are those Bible trivia and Bible jeopardy games out there, and we ought to be playing those games. Just like the kids who are playing basketball for fun, we are becoming skilled in His Word because it is a delight. What is really happening is that our sword is becoming familiar and natural in our hand. We are training our thoughts and body to work as a unit as we are wielding our sword. When our time comes to enter the battle, we will find that we are Sword masters ready to meet <u>all</u> challenges. Beloved, that is how it should be, that is how it can be.

Beloved, when we are in a battle and we are wielding our Sword, we have to do this with faith. We have to believe our Sword can defeat any and all challenges to it. I was in a trial once that pushed me to my extreme, or so I thought. Anyway, I knew that I was obeying what the Lord had told me to do; I asked the Lord to search my heart to make sure that nothing was in there to hinder the Holy Spirit. I was clean; I was in obedience; why was I in so much angst or in such an anxious state of mind? The Lord spoke to me and said that I needed to rest in my trust of Him. I knew I trusted the Lord and I did not understand why the Lord did not just charge in and smite my enemies.

I knew that He would work everything out - it was the "when" that was my primary concern for the moment. In my early morning time with Him that day, I had praised Him for all of His mercies that He had poured out on me in my life. I knew the Lord had always protected me and taken care of me. To make a short story even shorter, I rested. I did not understand a lot about the trial, it did hurt but I knew that whatever happened, *whether short or long,*

I could trust the Lord. He is out for my best interests and He had a solid track record to prove it.

In regards to my trial, I had to believe that no weapon formed against me would prosper whether that weapon was depression, slander or political office moves. I had to believe that my Sword was sharp enough to counter any challenge that would come its way. A couple of days later when that phase of the trial had ended and the Lord was faithful *as always,* I reflected on how foolish it is to wonder or even question God's Word. He is God after all. I can take my troubles to Him and He moves on my behalf – WOW!! I was humbled and grateful that He is really good and kind towards someone such as me. It is the same for you. He is good and kind and even though you may be in the midst of a painful trial right now, He will see you through and it will be for your good. His Sword can be trusted to stay sharp in the battle. He is trust*worthy.*

You may ask, "what does it mean to wield your Sword?" Well, I will give you some examples so you will understand. Let's take something simple, like a Bible study group. This group meets together once a week to learn and grow in the ways of the Lord. They all go to the same church and they all hunger after righteousness. Of course, there are different income levels, different family situations and different backgrounds, but that does not seem to matter; they are all serious about following after the Lord.

One of the sisters in the group gets offended by something that the leader of the study group says and, instead of dealing with it right then and there, the sister goes home and lets the offense fester and grow. This sister, who is young in the Lord, decides that the best thing for her to do is to leave the group. She calls the leader of the study group and says that she was offended and she will not be coming back. Of course the leader apologizes for any offense, but the sister is adamant that she will not be coming back.

At the next meeting of the study group, the leader shares the sad news with the rest of the group. So, how does the Sword get used in a situation like this? We have to recognize that this is a classic strategy that the enemy uses and, unfortunately, it is quite successful. Separate *a* sheep from the fold and they are vulnerable to be attacked. Most wolves will not attack a group. Okay, we know the enemy has helped with the separation; if the group goes after the separated one and not allow the separation, the wolf will have a very difficult time with the attack. Our response to this line of thinking might be, "if she wants to leave the group then there is nothing we can do to stop it."

This is the whole point, we can stop it; we take our Sword and slice – *we are all members of One body, if one part suffers, we all suffer.* We just do not allow the sister to leave the fellowship without a good fight. That may sound unconventional and it is certainly lacking in social etiquette, but the truth is that the sister is running from the Lord for whatever reason. If your spouse suddenly wanted to walk out of the marriage, I am sure you would not allow it without a mighty fight.

> *Who is My mother and who are My brothers?*
> *...whoever does the will of My Father who is in heaven,*
> *he is My brother and sister and mother. Mt. 12: 48-50*

You are not that popular at work. You are known as goody-two- shoes and most people regard you as different. You have learned to live with it and it really does not bother you. You are a serious Christian, you love the Lord and you do not hesitate to share about your Lord whenever a door opens.

One day in the office one of your more popular co-workers is telling a story that is full of sexual connotations and vulgar language. Everyone is laughing and you find yourself laughing too because after all, the story is funny and you don't want your co-workers to think of you as a total prude. The days and weeks go by and you find yourself laughing at more of *those* funny stories. Your thinking is that you are showing your co-workers that you *do* have a sense of humor.

What you don't know is that your co-workers need and want to see somebody different. They need to see how righteous people conduct themselves. Deep in their spirit they want to see someone living in the Truth. Your concern should not be what your co-workers think of you but what the Lord thinks of your actions. When the stories and jokes begin, take your Sword and slice – *love [you] does not rejoice in unrighteousness, but rejoices with the truth.* You force yourself to not even make a tiny smile because the truth is that what is happening is offensive to your Lord. That may turn you into a "kill joy" and you may have to endure even more unpopularity, but that is okay, you are supposed to be about your Father's business anyway; not trying to win a popularity contest. There are souls at stake.

> *How blessed is the man who does not walk in the counsel of the wicked, nor stand in the path of sinners, nor sit in the seat of scoffers. Ps. 1: 1*

As you can see, the Sword slices through those ungodly thoughts that we have throughout the day in the situations that we encounter. Left on our own, we would use the wisdom of the world and end up falling off the cliff.

Contend earnestly for the faith which was once for all delivered to the saints. If you do not contend for your faith, it will be destroyed. The enemy will not let you just go about your business and then retire in heaven. The Lord Himself said that in this world you will have tribulations. If you become handy with your Sword, you at least give as good as you get.

Knowing how to use your Sword can save you so much unnecessary pain. When you feel depressed, lonely, angry, confused, betrayed and hurt, those are the times when you are susceptible to the enemy whispering things into your mind. Knowing the Word will help you navigate through those storms instead of tossing about like a piece of driftwood. For those of us who know the Word, we still have to walk in the Word to keep a sharp Sword. Our minds can know a lot of Scripture but when we *experience* the Scripture - that is when the glory of fighting with a sharp Sword manifests itself.

Beloved, if the enemy can get us to put down our Sword, he has won a mighty victory. The enemy worries about the saints that believe and walk in the Word. The enemy does not worry over the saints that just have a ceremonial sword that they wear on Sundays or bring to the Bible Study. The big worry is over those saints that take it into the dark cesspools.

The Word will always do what it was sent to do. We know the Word was sent to set the captives free. If the Word is taken into a dark pit, it will set the captives free. All we have to do is speak the Word. By hearing the Word, His called will respond. I am not saying that we will have an instant revival (*of course you never know*) but all we have to do is to be obedient and the Word will do the rest. That is thrusting with the Sword!

If we all went into the dark cesspools such as the prisons, the bars, mental institutions, nursing homes, video arcades, striptease joints (*yes*), crack houses and street corners and we *just* spoke whatever the Holy Spirit gave us to speak we would very quickly see the God of all creation move on our behalf and His called would come. Churches would overflow.

The Lord says to go into the highways and byways and to beat the bushes so His house can be full. Beloved, the fear that stops us needs to be crushed. We do not have to wait until we have a passion for the lost; we just need to be obedient. We always talk about how the Lord is not doing miracles today like He used to do. Let's give Him something to work some miracles on. If you are not making headway on winning souls at work – go into the byways!

We all know there are plenty of lost people in the down and out part of town, let's go there. We all know where those "wild" teens hang out; let's go there. <u>Let's go where our Sword will do the most damage to the enemy.</u> The worst that can happen is that we will lose our life. The best that can happen is that we will *lose* our life.

Beloved, our comfort will come but, for now, let's get to work. I know some of us think that we have nothing to say to some of these lost people, but we all were lost at one point in our lives. That is sufficient enough, we know what it is like to grope about in the darkness, we know what it is like to drift about, and we know what it is like to not have the comfort of Jesus. Beloved, we know. We have something to say and people are waiting to hear. We do not have to be eloquent orators; we just have to be obedient. The Spirit will take care of the rest.

> *But Moses said to the sons of Gad and to the sons of Reuben, "Shall your brothers go to war while you yourselves sit here?" Num. 32:6*

He will not disappoint. He will not call us to do something and then just leave us hanging in the wind. The God we serve will do us right. He will show Himself mighty on our behalf. He will give us the words, the courage and the victory. He gave us the Sword so we could use it. It is not a ceremonial Sword. It is meant to conquer; it is meant to shatter chains; it is meant to break down walls; it is meant to set the captives free.

> *"When the Helper comes, whom I will send to you from the Father, that is the Spirit of truth, who proceeds from the Father, He will bear witness of Me, and you will bear witness also..." Jn. 15:26, 27*

Chapter Ten

Prayers With No Fluff

For it is not an idle word for you; indeed it is your life.
Deut. 32:47

Have you ever driven through a mountain pass at night? There is thick, pea soup fog. The fog just bounces back the light from your car headlights. It is hard to see the shoulder line on the road and you, very naturally and wisely, drive slower. You keep driving because you know that this road will take you to where you need to go. Every now and then, the fog suddenly clears and you can see everything clearly then it closes in again. Even though you can't see anything except what is directly in front of the car, you know that the planet is still there.

We are driving through the mountain pass. The fog of this world is thick as pea soup. You cannot see the Kingdom but you know it is there. All you can see is what is directly in front of you and it seems as if your light just bounces back at you. Every now and then, the fog clears and you can see the Lord and His Kingdom clearly and your spirit soars at the reality of it. And then, just as quickly, the fog closes back in and you begin to tell yourself again that the Kingdom is there - even though you can't see it.

That is the reality of this world. We really do see through a glass darkly and what we see is muted and distorted. One day the fog will be blown away and we will see His face clearly. We will be astounded that He is right in front of us and always has been. The truth is that He is closer than the air we breathe. Scripture says that the Spirit searches the deep things of God and our spirit is His lamp. If our spirit is *His* lamp, then there is nothing about us that is hidden. Nothing.

We may have things that have happened to us that have scarred or wounded us and the only way we know how to deal with them is to stuff them down and forget about them. The Lord knows about them. There may be things that have shamed us so deeply that they have caused us to take another track in life than the one that we were on originally. The Lord knows about that. We may have thoughts so perverted that they would make the average person get sick if you shared those thoughts with them. The Lord knows about that. Nothing is hidden. He is right there, seeing it all. Conversely, you could be sending money to some organization to feed the hungry because compassion touched your heart and you have shared this with no one. The Lord knows about them. It could be that when you make out your check to pay tithes that it will drop your savings down to zero. The Lord knows and sees your faith overcoming your anxiety.

That is what is so wonderful about serving the Lord. He knows everything. That is why He can answer our prayers before we even think about praying them; because He knows.

> *If I say, "Surely the darkness will overwhelm me, and the light around me will be night," even the darkness is*

not dark to You, and the night is as bright as the day.
Darkness and light are alike to You. Ps. 139: 11,12

We often equate the Lord's response to us by our goodness or sinfulness. When we are experiencing the intensity of His love for us, we often forget that when we do not feel anything, His love is still just as intense as when we can feel it. The fog swirls. Everything is the same. Our faith can take us through the fog, but often we panic.

When we kneel down to pray, we need to understand that the Lord is right there, whether we feel like He is listening or not. He is right there when we ramble on for others to see or hear. He is right there when we are saying words to slice our brother or sister and calling it a prayer. He is right there when our emotions are so strong about something we cannot find the words and all we can do is moan. He is right there as the fog swirls.

When we wake up in a cold sweat from a nightmare and we begin praying, He is right there to calm our spirit. When our husband or wife of 51 years gets diagnosed with Alzheimer's disease, He is right there to hear our cry. When we harden our heart against our son or daughter because they married outside of their race, He is right there. When we get mad at Him and decide to not talk to Him, He is right there. The fog is just fog and seeing is not believing.

Many saints have a hard time with prayer. It is easier to spend time with someone you can see or, at least, audibly hear. Many of us can spend hours on the phone sharing our lives and not spend ten minutes with our Lord that gives us that life. Fortunately, just as in the game of golf, the Lord gives us a handicap. He is called the Holy Spirit. He helps us to pray.

Those whisperings throughout the day that we constantly try to ignore, believe it or not, that's Him. When we come home from work dog-tired, and we glance at our Bible with a lack of enthusiasm, oh yes, that's Him. When we wake up in the middle of the night, wide-awake, guess what, that's Him. When we wake up an hour before the alarm goes off, you got it, that's Him. There is no such thing as a coincidence.

These are soft nudgings from the Holy Spirit calling us to prayer. If we are obedient, we go to prayer. When we get there, many of us just begin rambling or we sit quietly and fall asleep. We have to understand that He is right there; 'very near you, in your mouth and in your heart.'

If you believe this, you will come in respectful reverence. If you wanted to talk to your Dad, you would not come up to him and just begin rambling. You would wait until you got his attention and then begin having a *two-way* conversation. Many of us forget that the Lord is the one who designed us in His image. It would stand to reason that He can talk if we can. Hmm.

I would even be so bold as to propose that He has some things that He would like to say to us, individually.

Some of us say that we pray throughout the day, so, we do not have to spend a block of time with the Lord. I beg to differ. My best friend will testify to this: if we go a month with a bunch of one liners such as "hi," "how are you doing," "fine," "take care;" I am quickly on the phone with her telling her that we are drifting apart and that is unacceptable to me. How much more our Friend that sticks closer than a brother?

We need to spend a block of time with the Lord to establish a relationship with Him so when the fog swirls we know that He is still there. When we know Him, we want to spend a block of time with Him because He is great to spend time with. Contrary to popular opinion, He is not boring; in fact, He will show you what living is all about. They don't call Him Life for nothing.

Now, I am not saying that you have to spend a block of time with the Lord everyday or you will not get to know the Lord. I am not trying to bring condemnation or legalistic baggage to anybody. I think people bring their own judgments on themselves. If we meet someone and we want to get to know that person better, we usually try to spend more time with the person. If we want a deep, intimate relationship with that person we usually spend a lot more time with them. You might be the unusual person who is able to foster a deep relationship with someone by just saying "hi" and "bye." If that is the case, you are off the hook. For the rest of us, if we need to spend time with someone to foster a deep relationship, then it stands to reason that we cannot expect to have a deep relationship with the Lord unless we spend time with Him.

Most of us make prayer far more complicated than it really is. You share the things about your life with Him, such as your joys, hopes, fears and concerns and He shares things about His life with you. The more you share, the closer you get; the more you share, the closer you get; the more you share... you get the point. That is all prayer is; it is a way to communicate with our God. He is Spirit so we must communicate with Him in the Spirit. We must listen for Him in our spirit. He will speak to us through His Word, through circumstances, often through another brother or sister and often directly to our spirit. I have had many times when I needed Him to speak to me directly and instantly. The quickness of His response stunned me.

He is not trying to make this walk any harder than it already is. He has made it so basic we often miss it. For the saint that really latches on to prayer, they have achieved a major victory. If you remember, Jesus was in constant prayer during His time on earth, how much more should we be? The enemy knows 'that the prayer of a righteous man achieves much.' If the enemy can keep us from praying, he will keep us from gaining the victory. What follows is an excerpt from *Letter 4 of The Screwtape Letters by C.S. Lewis*. It is a fictional account of two demons discussing, via letters, about the best way to destroy a Christian. The Enemy in the story is, of course, God. Well, it is *supposed* to be fiction.

'The best thing, where it is possible, is to keep the patient from the serious intention of praying altogether. When the patient is an adult recently re-converted to the Enemy's party, like your man, this is best done by encouraging him to remember, or to think he remembers, the parrot-like nature of his prayers in childhood.

In reaction against that, he may be persuaded to aim at something entirely spontaneous, inward, informal, and unregularised; and what this will actually mean to a beginner will be an effort to produce in himself a vaguely devotional *mood* in which real concentration of will and intelligence have no part. One of their poets, Coleridge, has recorded that he did not pray "with moving lips and bended knees" but merely "composed his spirit to love" and indulged "a sense of supplication". That is exactly the sort of prayer we want; and since it bears a superficial resemblance to the prayer of silence as practiced by those who are very far advanced in the Enemy's service, clever and lazy patients can be taken in by it for quite a long time.

At the very least, they can be persuaded that the bodily position makes no difference to their prayers; for they constantly forget, what you must always remember, that they are animals and that whatever their bodies do affects their souls. It is funny how mortals always picture us as putting things into their minds: in reality our best work is done by keeping things out.

If this fails, you must fall back on a subtler misdirection of his intention. Whenever they are attending to the Enemy Himself we are defeated, but there are ways of preventing them from doing so. The simplest is to turn their gaze away from Him towards themselves. Keep them watching their own minds and trying to produce *feelings* there by the action of their own wills. When they meant to ask Him for charity, let them, instead, start trying to manufacture charitable feelings for themselves and not notice that this is what they are doing. When they meant to pray for courage, let them really be trying to feel brave. When they say they are praying for forgiveness, let them be trying to feel forgiven. Teach them to estimate the value of each prayer by their success in producing the desired feeling; and never let them suspect how much success or failure of that kind depends on whether they are well or ill, fresh or tired, at the moment.

But of course the Enemy will not meantime be idle. Wherever there is prayer, there is danger of His own immediate action. He is cynically indifferent to the dignity of His position, and ours, as pure spirits, and to human animals on their knees He pours out self-knowledge in a quite shameless fashion. But even if He defeats your first attempt at misdirection, we have a subtler weapon.

The humans do not start from that direct perception of Him, which we, unhappily, cannot avoid. They have never known that ghastly luminosity, that stabbing and searing glare which makes the background of permanent pain to our lives. If you look into your patient's mind when he is praying, you will not find *that*. If you examine the object to which he is attending, you will find that it is a composite object containing many quite ridiculous ingredients. There will be images derived from pictures of the Enemy as He appeared during the discreditable episode known as the Incarnation: there will be vaguer—perhaps quite savage and puerile—images associated with the other two Persons. There will even be some of his own reverence (and of bodily sensations accompanying it) objectified and attributed to the object revered. I have known cases where what the patient called his "God" was actually *located*—up and to the left at the corner of the bedroom ceiling, or inside his own head, or in a crucifix on the wall. But whatever the nature of the composite object, you must keep him praying to *it*—to the thing that he has made, not to the Person who has made him. You may even encourage him to attach great importance to the correction and improvement of his composite object, and to keeping it steadily before his imagination during the whole prayer. For if he ever comes to make the distinction, if ever he consciously directs his prayers "Not to what I think thou art but to what thou knowest thyself to be", our situation is, for the moment, desperate.

Once all his thoughts and images have been flung aside or, if retained, retained with a full recognition of their merely subjective nature, and the man trusts himself to the completely real, external, invisible Presence, there with him in the room and never knowable by him as he is known by it—why, then it is that the incalculable may occur. In avoiding this situation—this real nakedness of the soul in prayer—you will be helped by the fact that the humans themselves do not desire it as much as they suppose. There's such a thing as getting more than they bargained for!' *

I will not be so presumptuous as to improve or clarify on C.S. Lewis, but I hope you realize that the enemy has a strategy to defeat us. The Lord has a strategy to make us 'more than conquerors' but we must communicate with Him to get the strategy. Just because we put on the armor and hold the sword, that does not make us a warrior. We must have the mind of a warrior also, and the only place we will receive that is at His feet, in prayer.

The Lord is good to those who wait for Him, to the person who seeks Him. Lam. 3:25

The purpose of prayer is not just to communicate with God; it is also the place where God does a lot of His major work on us. It is the place where we come and present ourselves to Him with our defenses down. It is the place where we claim our rights as His children, His inheritance. This is the vehicle that Jesus' blood paid for so we could have a restored relationship with God. This is where the rubber meets the road. It is an absolutely priceless gift to be able to come to Him and spend time with Him. We are so far fallen we do not realize what an absolute miracle we walk in when we come into His presence. Remember, the Israelites could not even touch the mountain that the Lord was abiding on.

But you have come to Mount Zion and to the city of the living God, the heavenly Jerusalem, and to myriads of angels, to the general assembly and church of the first-born who are enrolled in heaven, and to God, the Judge of all, and to the spirits of righteous men made perfect, and to Jesus, the mediator of a new covenant, and to the sprinkled blood...

Let us therefore draw near with confidence to the throne of grace, that we may receive mercy and may find grace to help in time of need. Heb. 12: 22-24 and 4:16

When we first come to prayer, our mind is running nearly 100 miles per hour, thoughts are coming and going. As we kneel in His presence and concentrate on Him, on His works, on His love for us, on the price He paid for us, our mind begins to slow down. This does take practice but press on. As we continue to concentrate, we train our mind to focus on Jesus alone and nothing else. When that happens, we begin to understand why the Psalmist said, "in His presence is fullness of joy."

After we have quieted our minds, an amazing thing begins to happen; the Lord draws near and begins to share. He begins to unfold to us the riches of His wisdom. He unfolds the truth about the various things we are going through; remember we see through a glass darkly but His vision is clear.

Our opinions or thoughts that we have about various things begin to *adjust* to His way of thinking. Perhaps we want to know if we should try some endeavor that we have been tossing around in our mind. The Lord lets us know if He is pleased with it or not. Perhaps we have sinned and, even though we have asked forgiveness, we still feel guilty. The Lord may address that issue. He may convict us on something that we overlooked. He will address whatever is needful for the time. It is a holy and awesome time.

For his God instructs and teaches him properly. Isa.28:26

When we are in prayer and we do not "feel" any of this happening, do not fret or think that nothing is happening. This is where our faith comes in. The Lord has promised to finish the work that He has begun with us. He does not lie. As we spend more time with Him and in His Word, we will find ourselves beginning to see things the way He sees things. We will also begin to find ourselves getting to know Him. We begin to find out things that are on His heart; things that He is concerned about. I say again that the relationships that the Lord had with Abraham, Moses and Daniel are not exclusive; it all depends on how deep we want to go. Let us allow Him to 'lead us beside quiet waters.'

We do not have to keep our distance with God. We can be real. As we spend more time with Him, He will be faithful to *adjust* anything about our prayers that need adjusting. You may ask, "Why pray if God knows everything, anyway?" Just like all parents, He wants a partnership and He takes great delight when we come and talk things over with Him. He enjoys watching us process our ideas. He enjoys watching us grow into the fullness of His Son. He takes delight in everything about us. He loves us. What can I say; it is a pretty simple concept. Why does He love us? I don't know and it doesn't really matter. Let's just be thankful that He does and accept it. 'See to it that you do not refuse Him who is speaking.'

'Oh, the depth of the riches both of the wisdom and knowledge of God! How unsearchable are His judgments and unfathomable His ways! For who has known the mind of the Lord, or who became His counselor? Or who has first given to Him that it might be paid back to Him again? For from Him and through Him and to Him are all things. To Him be the glory forever. Amen.'

D.M. Carthern

Chapter Eleven

Tailwinds

And thus, having patiently waited, he obtained the promise. Heb.6:15

tail wind or **tail·wind** (tāl'wīnd') n. A wind blowing in the same direction as that of the course of an aircraft, a ship, or another vehicle.

Tailwinds for the saint are truly icing on the cake. After you have been obedient, after you have died to yourself, after you have been faithful to all that the Lord has asked of you in your trial, it begins to dawn on you that the trial is over. You understand that your faith has been tested and it has passed through the fire. Your strength has been tested and it has amazed you how much you have. You understand what James was talking about when he said, "to count it all joy" because nothing feels so good as being faithful to God.

After that euphoria begins to pass, you begin to notice how much ground you have gained in your walk. Things that used to be such a struggle, now, you breeze through. Things that you thought would never change about you, now, you are in wonderment at the changes in your desires. You realize that you have changed but you are not sure when or how.

While you were concentrating on getting through your trial, the Lord was taking care of all kinds of issues in your heart. Remember when you were a child and the doctor used to distract you while he stuck you with a needle? Obviously, the Lord had the thought first.

While we are in our trial, we are fighting for all we are worth to stay focused on the Lord and not the trial. We are battling and we are in battle mode. Even though it seems forever, the trial does end. All that dross (*excess junk*) that you have been carrying along with you is now gone and you are light as a feather. When the Spirit blows, you just go wherever He wants you to go.

> *...and when the ship was caught in it, and could not face the wind, we gave way to it, and let ourselves be driven along. Acts 27:15*

Isn't this what surrender is all about, anyway? You could be in a headwind or a tailwind depending on which way you are going. You obviously use less fuel and make better time going with the tailwind. Just make sure the wind blowing is the Spirit.

> *Although He was a Son, He learned obedience from the things which He suffered. Heb.5:8*

It would be nice if we could learn the things we needed to learn a different way, but it seems like affliction is the only thing that makes us focus on God, totally. If we learn to obey God, we find out that we live in a totally different world. It is not euphoria. It is not blessings forevermore. It is a world where you live raw. It is a world where nothing is hidden; there are no pretenses. It is a totally foreign world to mankind. It is a world where you are brutally honest with yourself because the Lord will have no shadows in His Kingdom. It is clear and refreshing.

It is a world where you learn not to question His judgment but you know that you can always appeal to His mercy. It is a world where you know nothing can happen to you without His say so. It is a secure world. It is a world where you know everything that happens to you is for your good. It is a world where trust is alive and well.

Suffering is a part of this world. If there were another way to learn, the Lord would be using it. When bad things happen, it does not mean the Lord is angry with us. On the contrary, the Lord disciplines those He loves. The things we have to learn even the angels desire to learn. He is rightly called the Pearl of *great* price. We are all being freely given the most precious thing in all of creation. We don't understand it now, we can't see it now, but when we see His face, we will understand the enormity of the gift. In the meantime, we suffer for a little while.

We have to understand that the Lord's love for us compels Him to push us down the aisle. If He did not spare His Son, He will not spare us. If we are one of the blessed ones to be predestined, then we were called. If we were called, then He justified us. If He went through all the pains to justify us, then He will absolutely glorify us. When we asked Jesus to come into our heart, we entered a binding agreement with Him that said that He could step into our lives and *re-create.* In the midst of our trials, we have probably often wondered what He was making over. But when we emerged from the trial victorious, I know we could feel the wind at our backs.

A tailwind is confidence in the work that the Lord has thus far worked in us. We *now* know what we are made of. We know we love and trust God. Of course, it can grow but we know that the little we have has been through the fire and 'it came forth like gold.' This is why the *proof* of our faith is far more precious than gold that perishes. The Lord and I, the Lord and you, we have an understanding. We did not desert. We trust Him and He knows it.

This is when it gets good. Now the Bible is something we read because our Friend, that we are getting to know very well, wrote it. We read it now because we do not want to disappoint. We read it now because we understand *all* we have to do is obey and we grow. How simple.

> *My sheep hear my voice, and I know them, and they*
> *follow me. Jn. 10:27*

As we go along with the Wind, we understand that we are very different. Prayer time is our refuge. Jesus is our Friend, often our only friend. For the first time, our spirit is leading our mind. We are tuned into the Lord's voice. Understand that this is a wonderful time and enjoy the time but the next trial *will* come. Remember, we go from faith to faith, strength to strength and glory to glory. When you begin to enter your next trial, do not think that you have done something wrong. It is part of our life in the Kingdom *in this age.*

There is a difference with the next trial, though; now we trust the Lord more, we understand what obedience means. We are more in tune with our spirit. Deep calls to deep. It will be a different trial. We will still crucify our flesh, we will still suffer but this time, we will count the suffering as small because we understand what the goal is. We may even be so bold as to embrace our trial. Well, you never know. We have endurance now and it will do nothing but grow. God will have His way with us. He has promised it.

I just want to say one more thing about tailwinds. If you do not keep your eye focused, you will find yourself going off course.

Remember to stay alert and to stay focused. We have an enemy out there roaming, looking for some saint that is blissfully dozing at the wheel. The enemy thought Job was an easy mark because the Lord had blessed him so much. Job was blessed but he was also alert and sober. He understood that he was just passing through.

Beloved, the object of the walk is not to see how many blessings we can obtain from the Lord before we die. The object of the walk is to walk in the fullness of what we were called to be. The enemy would like for us to never discover this. Along with this knowledge also comes the *certain* knowledge that the enemy is a defeated foe. There is nothing to fear with him; he is kaput; finito; like, blown away, man.

A tailwind should not be the biggest part of the walk; trials are. I know that is not a popular teaching, but it is the truth. Our Lord was the Suffering Servant. How much more should we be? If God took suffering away whenever we asked, we would follow him for comfort and convenience, not out of love and devotion.

When rough times and suffering come, we think of them as the abnormal part of the walk and as something to get through as quickly as possible - or there must be some way to manipulate the Lord into getting rid of this bad time. When we are being blessed, we often think of them as the way things are supposed to be. I would have to agree that they are more pleasant but we cannot have a steady diet of candy.

In a trial, our weakest part is exposed and we usually try to shore it up or keep it covered. The Lord is trying to teach us that in our weakest areas He does not want us to shore them up. He wants us to lean on Him. That is what the Lord meant when He told Paul that His grace is sufficient. Jesus will usually pull a ministry from our very weaknesses.

Moses was not confident in his speaking - to the point of stuttering - so what does the Lord do? He makes Moses His mouthpiece. Gideon had convinced himself that he was nothing - so what does the Lord do? He makes him a king. Isaiah felt that he was too great a sinner to do anything for the Lord - so what does the Lord do? He makes him a prophet of righteousness. Paul was a Pharisee of Pharisees and the Law meant everything - so what does the Lord do? He makes him a minister to a people without the Law. I am sure that rocked Paul's world.

The Lord makes us all a new creation and at our weakest point He will meet us and show forth His strength and glory, to the point that we can minister strength to others from that place. We need to glory in our weaknesses because that is where the best in us is able to shine and, truly, the best in us is the Lord Christ.

It is I who made the earth, and created man upon it.
For I am God, and there is no other; I am God, and
there is no one else like Me. Isa. 45:12, 46::9

Tailwinds are great but remember that they are just an interlude. It is a time to catch our breath and recheck our sails because the next storm is coming as sure as our Lord is coming. If we can understand this concept, we will enjoy the tailwinds that much more and take full advantage of them when we are experiencing them.

It is also a good time to examine where we are with the Lord. When we are in a trial, it is not the time to examine our walk or make big decisions. In the tailwinds, we have a tendency to see and think more clearly - not to mention, we tend to be in a more humble state of mind.

If we have examined ourselves correctly during the interlude, when the next trial comes, we should be just a little bit more stable.

Grain for bread is crushed, indeed, <u>he</u> does not continue to thresh it forever. Isa. 28:28

We serve a good God. He absolutely wants the best for us and He will not shirk His duty as our Shepherd. We must believe that. Oil cannot be brought forth from the olive without crushing it.

The branches of the wild olive tree are pretty stiff and it has a gnarled trunk. The leaves are leathery and the flowers are small. The fruits are large; it is the outer, fleshy parts of the fruit that yield the valuable olive oil. <u>Thirty-one percent</u> of the ripe fruit is oil. The ripe fruit is eaten raw, as is the green, unripe fruit. The wood of the trunk and limbs are hard. The tree grows very slowly, but it attains a great age. It is difficult to kill the olive tree by cutting it down, because new sprouts are sent up from the root and all around the outside of the old stump, often forming a grove of two to five trunks - all from a single root that *originally supported* only one tree! *

Saints, we are not trying to be the prettiest thing out there. We are trying to be a useful tool for the Master. Our goal is to be knarled, leathery, have plenty of oil, large fruits, hardened and very hard to kill. People should be getting us raw without any pretense. It is okay for them to see our weaknesses because then they will see when the Lord steps in to meet us. The world knows how to be *self*-sufficient. They need to see a God–sufficient person. Our "no" should be "no" and our "yes" should be "yes." Even if we should be cut down, our root is Jesus; we should have shoots going out everywhere. <u>That</u> is the church. <u>That</u> is a bride fit for the King of Kings!

We are not trying to "fit in;" we are supposed to be different. We may sometimes be called politically incorrect or we may be accused of spoiling the party. We are supposed to spoil the party. Certainly, many a time, we will feel like a doormat. Life would be so much easier if we just went with the flow, but if you really look at people, they are miserable and they spend their lives creating distractions from their misery. We have the answer. Nobody may want to hear it or like it, but it is still the answer.

They hate him who reproves in the gate, and they abhor him who speaks with integrity. Amos 5:10

The tailwind is a brief rest and that is all. Our rest will come later. When He breaks the blue, will He find us working hard or taking an extended rest break? There is a war going on and people are being taken captive everyday. Our view of life needs to be enlarged. We are taken care of - we need to grab someone else who needs to experience a rest.

Chapter Twelve

Lord, Hold the Sun!

Then all your people will be righteous; they will possess the land forever, the branch of My planting, the work of My hands, that I may be glorified. "The smallest one will become a clan, and the least one a mighty nation. I, the Lord, will hasten it in its time." Isa. 60:21,22

The Lord Almighty holds all power. All principalities and powers bow to Him. NOTHING happens without His okay. He has said to His bride that the war has been won, victory is in effect. What else do we need to hear or know to rock this world? Do we really seek approval from our fellow human beings that much?

Ephraim is oppressed, crushed in judgment, because he was determined to follow man's command. Hos. 5:11

Most of our snares and trials come because we do not believe and trust the Lord. He has told us the sky is blue - why do we insist that the sky is checkered? We need to look deep within ourselves and make up our minds who we are going to serve. Once we decide, we need to follow that decision through, wholeheartedly. If we are going to serve the enemy, then serve him with gusto. If we are going to serve the One True God, then we need to serve Him with everything we have and quit half-stepping. Let us set our jaw and fight. It is a long and grim fight but we need to quit being wimps about it. We need to quit whining every time we experience an uncomfortable situation. We were called to be great saints, warriors extraordinaire, *more* than conquerors; we are children of the Living God. We are priests, set apart and deeply loved by the High King.

> *"And it will come about in that day," declares the Lord, "that you will call Me Husband and will no longer call Me Master." Hos. 2:16*

He still asks the question that rings through the ages, "Where are you?" We need to give an answer. We can stand firm for political candidates or ideals. We can stand firm for our favorite sports team. We need to declare ourselves and stand firm for Someone much greater than all that. I know deep in my spirit that on that Day, when I see His face and I see Him in all His beauty, I will be ashamed that I did not do more for One so lovely. He has declared to us that He is not ashamed to call us His people. He has given His life for us. Are we so dysfunctional that we still turn our heads or keep our mouths closed in fear of being rejected by other clay vessels?

> *"Behold, those who wear soft clothing are in kings' palaces." Mt. 11:8*

Why did Jesus say that the poor have the Gospel preached to them? Why didn't Jesus just have His fisherman catch a bunch of fish and make a lot of money and give that to the poor? Why didn't He set up a fish and loaves kitchen? In fact, why didn't He heal everyone in Israel - or everyone on the planet?

The power, the hope, the joy, the freedom and the life are in the Word. Man needs nothing else except the Word. The enemy and our nature hate the Word. We have to understand that, in our natural makeup, we hate everything about God. In our natural essence, we will try every possible way to be God; the enemy will, too. This Word that carries life is able to take a person who is chained in the gutter with no hope and set them free with hope and a vision. This Word transforms the mind so that a person that relishes in their sin will turn their back on it and run after holiness. When we grasp the power that is in the Word and we understand that the Word lives in us, we will kick in the gates of Hell and march in. But we will not be popular walking on that path. We will probably not have many friends, if any.

Everyone knows this - that is why there is such a stigma with Christianity. Everyone knows the truth deep down in his or her spirit. Everyone knows there is a price to pay for walking that path. That is why there are so few people who walk it. Martin Luther was excommunicated. Dietrich Bonhoeffer had to go against the whole German church. These were men that became hard, leathery and knarled for God and when they were cut down, the sprouts went everywhere.

What will happen when we get cut down? Oh yes, we will be cut down. Will there be sprouts where we were planted? Does the enemy think we are worth cutting down? Is this life so precious that we would rather live on milquetoast or can we handle the meat? Beloved, we were called to be giants and we are living like ants.

"Behold, I am coming quickly, and My reward is with me, to render to every man according to what he has done." Rev. 22:12

What did Moses see that he walked away from the riches and prestige of Egypt to join a people that were slaves? What did Noah hear that he would build a boat, preach and be ridiculed for 120 years? What did Jeremiah know that caused him to endure being despised by his whole nation most of his lifetime? What was Hosea thinking when he went to marry a prostitute to start a family?

...and others experienced mockings and scourgings, yes, also chains and imprisonment. They were stoned, they were sawn in two, they were tempted, they were put to death with the sword; they went about in sheepskins, in goatskins, being destitute, afflicted ill-treated (men of whom the world was not worthy), wandering in deserts and mountains and caves and holes in the ground. Heb. 11: 36-38

These are our brothers and sisters. They were men and women who turned their backs on the world and gave the enemy a good fight. Warriors all. This is the legacy that we are called to. They were dust just like us. They did five things that pleased the Lord immensely and we will please Him also if we do the same:

1. **Put on the armor**
2. **Stand firm**
3. **Be on the alert**
4. **Pray for the other saints**
5. **Speak boldly**

The only thing that made them do the extraordinary was their hope in Jesus. We hope in Him, too.

We are called to do the extraordinary; Jesus did the extraordinary and we are called to follow Him. Jesus says the world was not worthy of them. Now they are worthy to judge the holy angels that stand in the presence of God.

Great Light, Mover of all that is moving and at rest, be my Journey and my far Destination, be my Want and my Fulfilling, be my Sowing and my Reaping, be my glad Song and my stark Silence. Be my Sword and my strong Shield, be my Lantern and my dark Night, be my everlasting Strength and my piteous Weakness. Be my Greeting and my parting Prayer, be my bright Vision and my Blindness, be my Joy and my sharp Grief, be my sad Death and my sure Resurrection! *

For those of us in the Kingdom, there is no other choice and there is no other way. True, we may not be called to such a walk as these great saints. Our calling might be to just make sure that our co-worker hears the Word, but that is no less significant. We still need to set our jaw, firm up our spine, slap the enemy out of the way and share the Word with our co-worker.

Ananias just had to be obedient in one thing; he had to go lay hands on a brother that had just been saved. It was a small thing. Once Ananias found out who the brother was, he tried to back out of it. Imagine how the New Testament would be if Ananias was disobedient. Never discount what our Lord asks us to do. We do not see the big picture. I am sure every soul that the Apostle Paul won to the Kingdom, Ananias got a little piece of that reward. We are called to do extraordinary things, even if it is just a simple thing like laying hands on a young brother.

Stephen was just a faithful brother serving the saints. He was so faithful; his local church made him a deacon. He continued to serve faithfully in season and out of season. When asked, he gave a reason for his faith that eventually cost him his life. As he was dying, he finally saw with his eyes the face of his Beloved and he was lit up. You cannot tell me that Stephen's act of being faithful *to the end* did not work on the heart of the soon to be Paul. Stephen was just being faithful. God was providing the powerful witness. So it is with us. We just have to be faithful and God will take care of the rest. That alone will allow us to walk in the extraordinary. That alone will cause the enemy to flee. Even when he thinks he has gained a victory the Lord turns it to his loss.

Every human that is not in the Kingdom is a prisoner. Whether you believe it or not, whether they believe it or not; it is true. Maybe you can't see or feel a person's chains. Maybe they appear to you to have it all - fame, power, riches and beauty, but that is a deception. Maybe they appear to you to have a great family life and a wonderful spouse and kids, but that is a deception. Pray for wisdom and discernment. Even if you can't see the chains, trust that the Lord does not lie. Everyone has fallen; everyone is a captive until Jesus sets them free. Pray and act accordingly.

There is a battle going on and we must fight for those that cannot fight for themselves. Most people don't even know that they are chained. I never knew darkness until I saw the Light. Nobody could have convinced me that I was in rags until the Spirit, in His compassion, sent someone to tell me. Pick up your Sword and fight. The enemy is just using smoke and mirrors.

Those who see you will gaze at you, they will ponder over you, saying, 'Is this the man who made the earth tremble, who shook kingdoms, who made the world like a wilderness and overthrew its cities, who did not allow his prisoners to go home?' Isa.14: 16,17

The enemy is just a created being like the rest of us. Oh yes, he and his cronies are cunning and they have been given a measure of authority but, just like the archangel Michael, we can say, "The Lord rebuke you" and they must go. We are sons and daughters of the Living God and there is no one higher. The weapons the Lord has given us have never known defeat. We will have the enemy running from us as we go about breaking the chains. We will soon see the enemy bow his knee to our Lord and to His inheritance, us.

Joshua was leader of the Israelites when he and the leaders of Israel agreed to protect the Hivites that lived in Gibeon. That agreement was given because the leaders of Israel and Joshua were deceived and they did not seek the Lord's counsel before giving their word. Nevertheless, the leaders gave their word and no matter what the circumstances, they had to keep it. Five other kings in the area got together and conspired to go to war against the Hivites in Gibeon. They were angry because the Hivites made peace with Joshua instead of banding with them to conquer the Israelites.

The men that lived in Gibeon immediately sent word to Joshua saying that these kings had come to make war against them and that Joshua should not abandon *his servants*. Joshua and the Israelites came to the rescue for no other reason except that they gave their word to the Hivites. On that famous day when Joshua asked the Lord to hold the sun so that the Israelites could finish fighting their enemies, it was not done to rescue friends or family. It was done to protect a people that had been deceptive towards them.

Joshua was a warrior who spent his whole life fighting to set people free. He knew no other way to function; he just set his jaw and went forward. If there was an obstacle in his way, he called on the Lord to take care of the obstacle - even if it was something as small as the sun going down.

Joshua conquered thirty-one kings in the Promised Land. The book of Joshua is a quick read but it took Joshua five <u>long</u> years to conquer those kings. I am sure there were times when Joshua was tired, depressed, not in the mood, scared; all the emotions that you would feel in a five year span fighting a war. He was just like you and me. All of these people mentioned in the Bible are not any different than you or me. We serve the same God and the same Holy Spirit goes before us. There is one faith, one God, one Spirit for all the saints. They entered a binding agreement with God. This is not about emotions - it is about commitment. The only power we have is over our will.

> *He who overcomes, I will grant to him to sit down with Me on My throne, as I also overcame and sat down with My Father on His throne. Rev.3:21*

We need to cry out with Joshua, 'Lord, hold the sun!' He will listen; the prisoners are waiting, creation is waiting. He is waiting for us to give the war cry.

THE END

BIBLIOGRAPHY

Except where noted *Master Study Bible*,New American Standard, Holman Bible Publishers, La Habra, CA, 1981.

Webster's 9th New Collegiate Dictionary, Merriam-Webster, copyright 1983, pg. 933.

Orson Welles, *War of the Worlds*, (transparencynow.com, 1996-2000), Ken Sanes

Olive Tree excerpt taken from *Ilumina Gold Bible Companion Text*, Tyndale House Publishers, Inc.,Wheaton, IL, 2003

Stephen R. Lawhead, *Merlin: Book Two of the Pendragon Cycle* (New York: Avon Books, 1988), pg.210

Denise. M. Carthern
email: dcarthern@comcast.net

Denise Carthern is available for speaking engagements and personal appearances. For more information contact:

Denise. M. Carthern
email: dcarthern@comcast.net

To order additional copies of this book or to see a complete list of all **ADVANTAGE BOOKS™** visit our online bookstore at:

www.advbookstore.com

or call our toll free order number at: 1-888-383-3110

Longwood, Florida, USA

"we bring dreams to life"™
www.advbooks.com

Printed in the United States
115375LV00002B/124-132/A